THE WORLD'S MOST FAMOUS

MARATHONS

RUNNING ON 5 CONTINENTS

© 24 ORE Cultura srl, Milan
Original title: Il Giro del mondo in 30 corse
ISBN 978-88-6648-212-3

Graphic design and layout: Pepe nymi, Milan
Image research: Valentina Minucciani

© of the English edition: h.f.ullmann publishing GmbH
Translation from Italian: Mark Eaton (marathon PB 2:45:06)
for Scriptum, Rome
Editing: John Gaunt in association with First Edition Translations Ltd,
Cambridge, UK
Typesetting: The Write Idea in association with First Edition
Translations Ltd, Cambridge, UK
Project management for h.f.ullmann: Lars Pietzschmann
Cover photos:
© istockphoto/stefanschurr(background);
© istockphoto/Leontura (skyline);
© Nic Bothma/epa/Corbis (runner)

Overall responsibility for production: h.f.ullmann publishing GmbH,
Potsdam, Germany

Printed in Germany, 2015

ISBN 978-3-8480-0831-5

10 9 8 7 6 5 4 3 2 1
X IX VIII VII VI V IV III II I

www.ullmann-publishing.com
newsletter@ullmann-publishing.com
facebook.com/ullmann.social

THE WORLD'S MOST FAMOUS

MARATHONS

RUNNING ON 5 CONTINENTS

by **ENRICO AIELLO**

with a foreword by
GIUSEPPE CRUCIANI

illustrations by
FEDERICA BROTTO

h.f.**ullmann**

CONTENTS

I RUN THEREFORE I AM

I did try to stop once. At first I felt free again. No more getting up at six in the morning, no more Sunday mornings grinding out miles and getting home shattered, with my legs aching and my brain addled. There was no longer any pleasure in it. I made the decision when I hit the 30-kilometer mark in the Reggio Emilia Marathon in December 2012, a wonderful course past fields and snow-covered hills, but suddenly the road ahead had become a nightmare. I had run out of steam, and anyone who has run a marathon will know what I mean. I had nothing left, so I told my running mate to carry on at his own pace. He sped off, and I was left like a block of marble. In the last twelve kilometers I walked, jogged a bit, tried to start running again, but every time I had to stop. I cursed every inch of the road. And above all I felt depressed. What am I doing here? Why do I make myself do it? It has always been difficult to explain that to normal people, who look at you as though you were mad when you go home early on Saturday night because you have to do twenty miles the next morning, on your own. It's like a duty, even though no one is paying you. The fact is that suddenly nothing else exists: your family, partner, friends. I once fell off my scooter and the first thing I thought was not that I might have died. No, I was just annoyed that I would have to miss a few months' training. Pure madness, you might be thinking. But this is what happens. The only thing that counts is training

schedules and your target—to complete a marathon. Running is pure selfishness, let's be honest. A crazy, wonderful form of selfishness. You set out with the top athletes, and when does that happen in any other sport? The adrenaline makes you feel alive, makes you feel you own the city. And as you run there is nowhere to escape from your weaknesses and your limits. You summon up your last reserves of energy, and you feel as happy as a lark. There is nothing rational in all this. I tried to do without it. For a year. Then I started again and I realized: I run therefore I am.

PS. I've always hated the New York Marathon. Jet lag; endless transfers; alarm at 4 o'clock in the morning; too much noise on the streets; and ugly, anonymous buildings. Compare that to the finish in Piazza Santa Croce in Florence. Or running through the crowds at the Trevi Fountain. There's no contest, believe me.

GIUSEPPE CRUCIANI

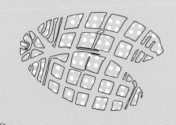

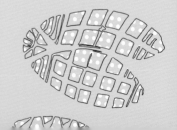

ABOUT THIS BOOK

Thirty races. Thirty locations all over the world, thirty experiences with one thing in common: the thrill of lining up before a race. True, runners are quite happy with a few miles in the local park; in fact this is when they often turn in their best performances. But no one would deny the special feeling you get from running in other cities, or surrounded by the beauty of nature. In short, running is a great way to explore the world, whether with a group of friends or on your own. Of my 24 marathons, for example, many have been planned and run together with friends. Few experiences can make you feel as close to people as training for months for the same goal, traveling and performing all the usual prerace rituals together (picking up race packs, pasta in the evening followed by a quick walk, jokes and pranks back at the hotel to relieve the tension, and then problems getting to sleep) and finally lining up with thousands of other people in the start zone, waiting for the starter's gun, after which everyone is on their own. A whirlwind of indelible sensations that we guard jealously, made up of memories, photos, medals, anecdotes, companionship, and passport stamps, in which everything merges into a single emotion. This is the social side of running.

Then there is another side, more personal but equally intense, which makes us want to live the whole race experience on our own. The journey, alone by choice, with our doubts and our hopes: the loneliness of the

long-distance runner, we might say. If I close my eyes I can still see my kit carefully set out on the other bed, the night before the race, with my number already pinned to my vest, and my gels all lined up. Then the ritual of putting on my running gear, hoping that I haven't forgotten anything, and finally the race, with only my thoughts for company.

This, then, is the spirit of this book: an invitation to set off and explore yourself as you explore distant places. No doubt you're wondering whether I've run all these races myself. The answer is no, not all of them. But I have run many of them, some as part of my job as a sports journalist, some purely for fun. And I am happy that I still have a lot of flags to plant, because this means I can still make plans and dream. And because the world is full of places that have yet to see me run. As for you, whatever your next destination I hope that every journey and every race will be an opportunity to look around you. And maybe also to look inside yourself.

Happy running!

ENRICO AIELLO

THE BIG
CHILL

"Adventure-seekers of the world, unite!"—you might be tempted to say. Running 21 kilometers in the darkness of the polar night, at a freezing latitude, might well seem like pure madness. But although it takes place in Tromsø on the 70th parallel north, the Polar Night Half Marathon is actually not just for the foolhardy! Challenging, obviously, and you need the right shoes and clothing, but less extreme than you might imagine. To that extent for many people it features on the growing list of "must-do" runs, an increasingly popular form of sports tourism that to my mind can only be a good thing. The truth is that running during the polar night—a phenomenon that envelops the area around the arctic polar circle in almost permanent darkness from November to January—has its own special charm. If you're wondering whether there is a race that celebrates the opposite phenomenon, the polar day, or midnight sun, the answer is obviously yes—the Midnight Sun Marathon, which is run on 21 June, also in Tromsø, an equally unusual and fascinating experience. But that's another story.

Opposite:
Aerial view of Tromsø, with the bridge linking the city to the mainland.

On pages 20–21:
The incredible spectacle of the aurora borealis seen from Grøtfjord.

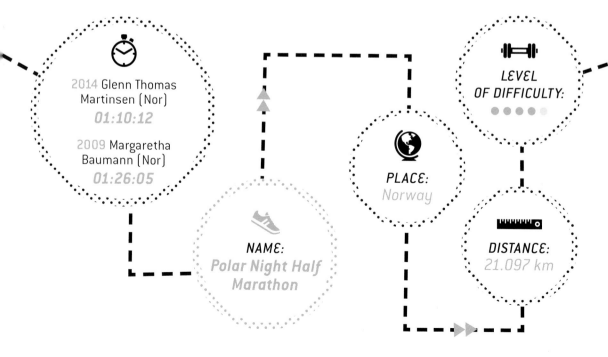

2014 Glenn Thomas Martinsen (Nor)
01:10:12

2009 Margaretha Baumann (Nor)
01:26:05

NAME:
Polar Night Half Marathon

PLACE:
Norway

LEVEL OF DIFFICULTY:
●●●●○

DISTANCE:
21.097 km

The start and finish lines of the Polar Night Half Marathon are on the main street in Tromsø, Storgata, and the race begins at 3 o'clock in the afternoon. The out-and-back route follows the coast toward the airport before turning back toward the town center. Being a night race (with three distances: half marathon, 10k, and 5k), runners are more concerned with staying on the road than admiring the scenery. Fortunately, if the weather allows it, the course is marked with burning torches to guide the runners, who are made even more visible by reflective vests (compulsory for safety reasons). The temperature is cold and the roads are icy, so don't forget to take the right shoes and clothing—thermal top and tights, hat and gloves, and especially shoes with spikes or grips. All in all, it's cold and it's tough, but the post-race party will warm you up and make it all feel worthwhile.

- -

1 Tromsø Lufthavn, Langnes

2 Tromsø Domkirke (cathedral)

3 Nordnorsk Kunstmuseum

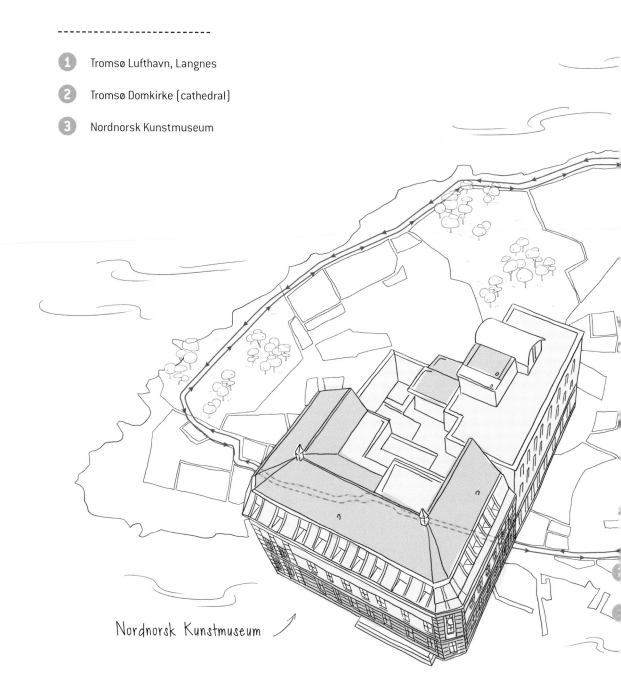

Nordnorsk Kunstmuseum

Tromsø Lufthavn
Lagnes

Tromsø Domkirke

MARATHON
HISTORY AND LEGENDS

The marathon, the ultimate athletics event, has its legends, its heroes, and its icons, both ancient and modern. If you've missed the last one hundred years (and more), here is a brief recap.

PHILIPPIDES OR PHEIDIPPIDES?

No one knows exactly. Just as it now seems certain that the well-known story of the messenger who collapsed after running from Marathon to Athens to deliver news of a military victory against the Persians belongs more to legend than to history. The alternative, and more probable, story is that he ran the 240 kilometers from Athens to Sparta (and the same distance back!) to ask Sparta for help and to report back to the Athenian general Miltiades.

Philippides or Pheidippides?
490 BC

DRAMA AT THE FINISH.

London 1908. A few hundred meters from the finish of the Olympic Marathon, one of the most dramatic episodes in the history of sport unfolded. The Italian Dorando Pietri, after collapsing several times inside the stadium, finished the race in first place. But as he had been helped up by the umpires, he was disqualified. In the stands (and not on the track, as is mistakenly believed) was Arthur Conan Doyle, who had been commissioned by the *Daily Mail* to write a report on the race.

26.385

At the same Olympics the marathon distance was increased to 26 miles 385 yards, which from then on became the standard length. Why? To allow the family of the Duchess of York, the future queen, to watch the start of the race from Windsor Castle, the summer residence of the Royal Family.

EMIL THE TERRIBLE

The 1952 Olympic Games in Helsinki are best remembered for the Czechoslovak runner Emil Zatopek. Shy and kind-natured, his running style was awkward, though highly effective. He achieved a quite remarkable feat, winning gold medals in three events: the 5,000 m, the 10,000 m and the marathon.

A MARATHON GOD

Athens Olympic Games, 2004. Stefano Baldini wins the gold after a tenacious, tactically perfect run. The whole nation is watching in excitement, suffering and celebrating together with their hero. The final moments, as he crosses the line on the black track in the Panathinaiko stadium, arms aloft, will be etched forever in the collective memory.

THE GREATEST OF THEM ALL

She holds the women's marathon world record, set in London on 13 April 2003 with a time of 2:15:25. She is a three-time winner of both the London Marathon and the New York Marathon, and won gold at the 2005 World Championships in Helsinki. Yet during her long career Paula Radcliffe, born in England in 1973, has never won a medal on the Olympic stage.

BAREFOOT IN THE DARK

The symbol of the 1960 Olympic Games in Rome is undoubtedly Abebe Bikila, an Ethiopian athlete who came to the marathon as an unknown at a time when the event was still dominated by Western runners. When he crossed the finish line at the Arch of Constantine in first place, he was probably not aware that he would be the forerunner of a generation of African champions who were inspired by his victory. What made his feat all the more memorable was the spectacular backdrop of torch-lit streets—the race was run in the evening to avoid the summer heat—and Bikila's unprecedented decision to run barefoot to tackle the uneven surface of the Roman Via Appia Antica.

AFRICAN DOMINATION

In the last 15 years the marathon has meant Algeria, Morocco, and above all Kenya and Ethiopia. From Haile Gebrselassie (world record-holder for many years) to Paul Tergat, Martin Lel, Kenenisa Bekele, and many others, a wave of African runners has flooded the starting lines of marathons all over the world. The current record (2:02:57) belongs to the Kenyan Dennis Kimetto, set on 28 September 2014 at the Berlin Marathon.

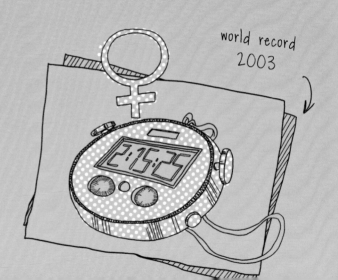

world record
2003

A RACE
FOR
"UNARMED SAMURAI"

If, like me, you feel irresistibly attracted to everything that is the opposite of you, if *Lost in Translation* is one of your favorite films, if you find the alienating atmosphere of Shibuya almost magnetic, then the Tokyo Marathon is the race for you. A member since 2013 of the World Marathon Majors, a series consisting of six of the largest and most renowned marathons in the world, Tokyo now has a huge field of 36,000 runners, and if it is so popular there must be a reason. Let's be honest, we Westerners are both disoriented and fascinated by a culture so different from our own, which despite its modern face still clings to ancient traditions. The race, incredibly well organized, as you would expect from the Japanese, will allow you to soak up this atmosphere. As you wait on the starting line, remember the definition of marathon runners coined by the Italian writer Mauro Covacich: "samurai without swords." This, after all, is what we are: samurai with running shoes.

Opposite:
Start of the 2014 edition. Over 1.7 million spectators line the route to cheer on the runners.

On pages 28–29:
Just before the start, in front of the Tokyo Metropolitan Government Building. According to the official race statistics, women make up 20% of entrants.

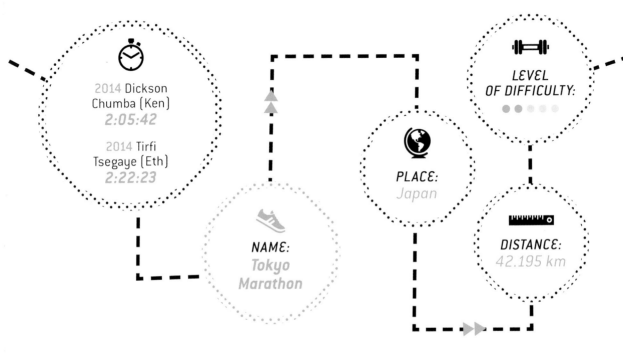

2014 Dickson Chumba (Ken)
2:05:42

2014 Tirfi Tsegaye (Eth)
2:22:23

NAME:
Tokyo Marathon

PLACE:
Japan

LEVEL OF DIFFICULTY:
● ● ● ○ ○

DISTANCE:
42.195 km

The Tokyo Marathon route is almost completely flat, even downhill for the first five kilometers or so, with just a couple of short uphill stretches toward the finish. The race sets off at just after 9 am, opposite the Tokyo Metropolitan Government Building, one of the most distinctive buildings in the financial district, and finishes at Tokyo Big Sight, a major convention center. En route you will get enthusiastic support from almost two million spectators. Highlights along the course include the Imperial Palace, at around kilometer 10; then Hibiya Park; the Tokyo Tower, 333 meters tall with fantastic observation decks; the districts of Ginza, with its distinctive architecture, Nihombashi, and—before kilometer 30—Asakusa with the Kaminarimon Gate, the entrance to the oldest Buddhist temple in Tokyo. The average temperature in February is around seven degrees, just below the ideal. Time limit: 7 hours.

----

1   Metropolitan Government Building

2   Imperial Palace

3   Tokyo Tower

4   Asakusa Kaminarimon Gate

5   Tokyo Skytree

6   Ginza 4-Chome Intersection

7   Big Sight

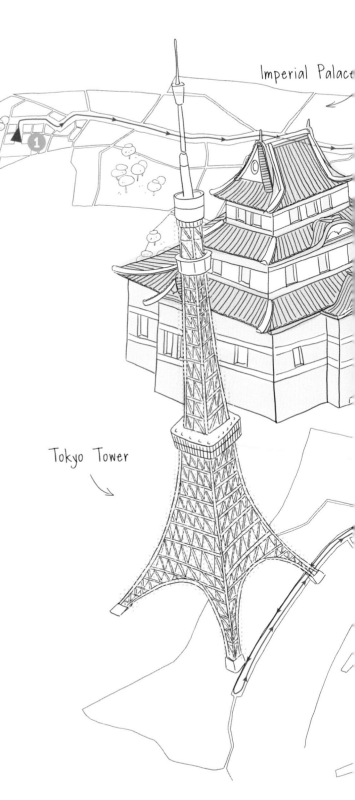

Imperial Palace

Tokyo Tower

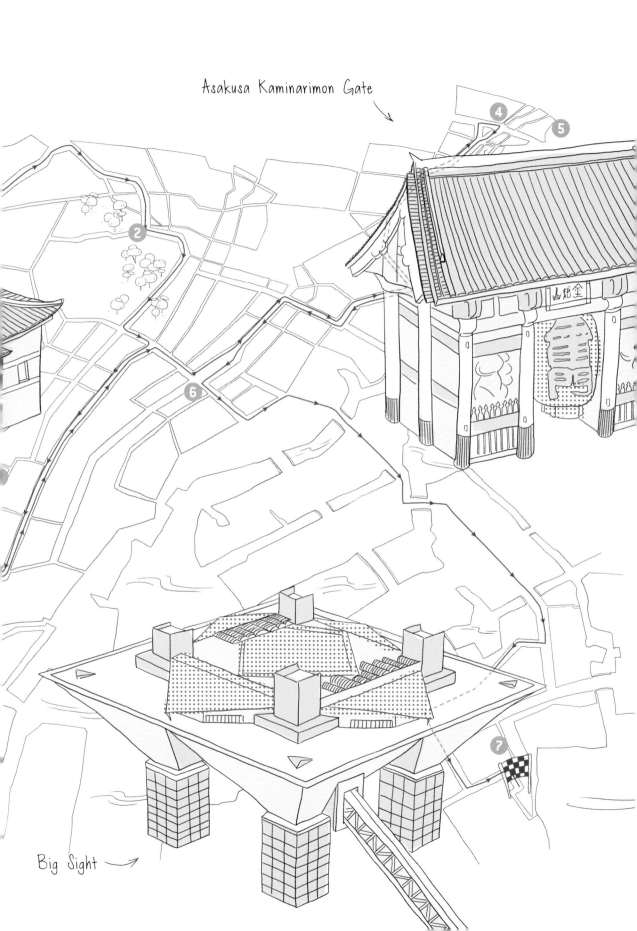

Asakusa Kaminarimon Gate

Big Sight →

A HALF
MARATHON
WITH PESTO

Take two beautiful, typically Italian resorts, a bit old-fashioned, perhaps, but still blessed with unique charm. Imagine a route from one to the other, with breath-taking views along the way. And if you missed anything the first time, repeat the whole experience. The result is the perfect recipe for a spectacular half mara-thon which for many runners marks the beginning of the running season after the rigors of winter. Running between Santa Margherita Ligure and Portofino is a special way to appreciate the beauty and the perfumes of the Gulf of Tigullio, a 21-kilometer treat for the eyes. If you're lucky enough to get a nice day for it (and chances are fairly good) you're very likely to make it an annual appointment in your running calendar—if only for the plate of *trenette al pesto* you get after the race, another very good reason for taking part!

Opposite:
The spectacular view over the Gulf of Tigullio, in itself an excellent reason to run this half marathon.

On pages 34–35:
A scene from the race, an out-and-back stretch of coastline from Santa Margherita to Portofino which runners have to cover twice.

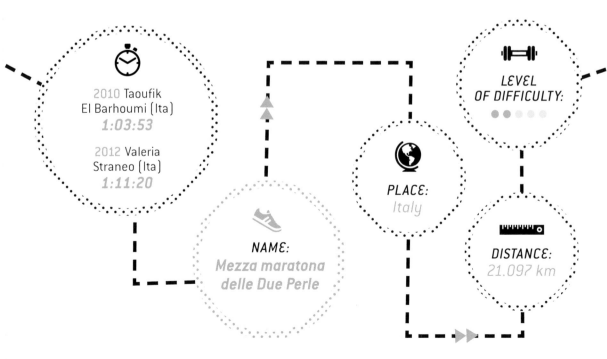

2010 Taoufik
El Barhoumi (Ita)
1:03:53

2012 Valeria
Straneo (Ita)
1:11:20

NAME:
*Mezza maratona
delle Due Perle*

PLACE:
Italy

LEVEL
OF DIFFICULTY:
● ● ● ● ●

DISTANCE:
21.097 km

1. Santa Margherita Ligure

2. Piazzetta di Portofino

3. Portofino

Piazzetta
di Portofino

From Santa Margherita to Portofino and back, twice. Two laps, setting out at 9 am from Piazza Martiri della Libertà in Santa Margherita Ligure and finishing in Portofino, winding along the coast road that links the two resorts. The double out-and-back formula—in other words the same stretch repeated four times—might make you think that the race is boring. You would be completely wrong. Running by the sea, with beautiful views over the Gulf of Tigullio—the stretch above the Paraggi beach is especially spectacular—make each five kilometer leg a real pleasure. Not forgetting that while you're running the first lap you'll meet the frontrunners coming the other way, which doesn't happen often during a race. The route has lots of bends and is slightly undulating, which means it's not the ideal race to go for your half marathon personal best. The only slight stumbling block is in Portofino, where you meet a series of narrow cobbled streets, so it gets a bit crowded and you have to watch where you put your feet, as well a short climb on your way out of the village.

PORTOFINO

CLOTHING:
DO THE RIGHT THING

Running apparel has evolved rapidly over the last few years. Nowadays materials are increasingly "intelligent," able to trap heat, which is crucial during the winter months, and to let your skin breathe. The result is a generation of thin, lightweight clothes that can help you maintain the perfect body temperature. And that look good, too, which is no bad thing.

USE TECHNICAL MATERIALS

Leave your sweatshirts and cotton T-shirts at home—they won't protect you from the rain and they get wet and heavy with sweat. Unless you want to catch a cold, but in that case don't blame running! Instead of cotton, choose clothes in technical materials, which have no stitching, protect you from the cold, and wick perspiration away from your skin.

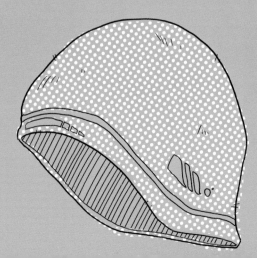

DON'T PILE ON HEAVY CLOTHES IN WINTER

Am I wearing enough? This is the doubt that besets runners, especially inexperienced runners, before training runs or races. Take a tip from me: remember that after you've been running for ten minutes you'll feel a lot hotter than you did when you set out. So don't cover yourself up too much. Don't forget to wear a technical vest, and above all protect those parts of the body that are most susceptible to heat loss, such as the neck, the ears and the hands.

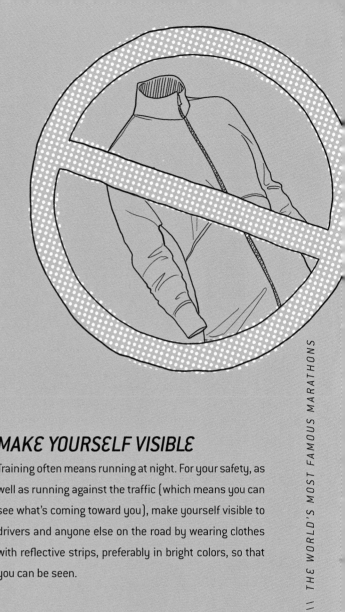

MAKE YOURSELF VISIBLE

Training often means running at night. For your safety, as well as running against the traffic (which means you can see what's coming toward you), make yourself visible to drivers and anyone else on the road by wearing clothes with reflective strips, preferably in bright colors, so that you can be seen.

DON'T SUFFER NEEDLESSLY IN HOT WEATHER

Unfortunately, you still see a lot of people running in the summer with long pants and wind jackets. The idea is to sweat as much as possible and lose weight. But this is not only ineffective, it's also dangerous, for the only thing you lose is body fluid, with a serious risk of dehydration and heatstroke. So give up the idea of subjecting your body to this pointless form of torture, and just enjoy your run!

RUNNING THROUGH
THREE THOUSAND YEARS
OF HISTORY

Whatever your views on the subject, you have to agree that few places in the world can inspire religious feelings like Jerusalem. It may be the presence of the symbols of three important religions; it may be because of its immense historical, cultural, and religious significance. Whatever the case, there can be no denying that that everything in this city takes on a powerful symbolic value. In a city like this, where an obsession with security does not stop people wanting to enjoy themselves, where in order to control the Arab sector the authorities could find no better solution than to build a wall, the annual marathon becomes a cry for freedom and an opportunity for exchange that attracts an increasing number of runners from all over the world. Everyone who has taken part will tell you that it is impossible to cross the old city or look up toward the Mount of Olives without thinking about what happened here just over two thousand years ago.

Opposite:
A highly symbolic shot of a marathon runner crossing the Old City with Israeli and Palestinian flags. Over 15,000 people from 50 countries take part in the event, which also includes a half marathon.

On pages 42–43:
At around kilometer 23 the course passes the Mount of Olives, where the Catholic Church of Dominus Flevit stands next to the Russian Orthodox Church of Mary Magdalene.

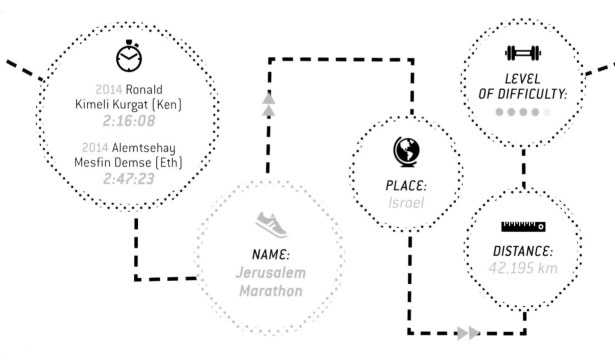

2014 Ronald Kimeli Kurgat (Ken)
2:16:08

2014 Alemtsehay Mesfin Demse (Eth)
2:47:23

NAME:
Jerusalem Marathon

PLACE:
Israel

LEVEL OF DIFFICULTY:

DISTANCE:
42.195 km

The Jerusalem Marathon is run on Friday, the day before the Jewish Sabbath, together with the half marathon, 10k and 5k races. Runners set off at 7 am—the heat and humidity are unforgiving—from Ruppin Boulevard, at the intersection between the Knesset (the Israeli parliament) and the Museum of Israel, and reach the finish line at the southern end of Sacher Park, after entering the city through a tunnel. At kilometer 10 you pass the Great Synagogue, and shortly after, at around kilometer 13, you catch your first glimpse of the Old City, where you return from kilometer 23, past the Jaffa Gate and the Zion Gate (which leads to Mount Zion, the site of the tomb of King David), the Mount of Olives and, at around kilometer 24, the Tower of David. The route is by no means flat, but then what matters here is not your personal best, but enjoying the unique sense of history that surrounds you. Time limit: 6 hours.

1 Mamilla Avenue
2 Jaffa Street
3 Jaffa Gate
4 Tower of David
5 Old City
6 Great Synagogue
7 Zion Gate
8 Mount of Olives

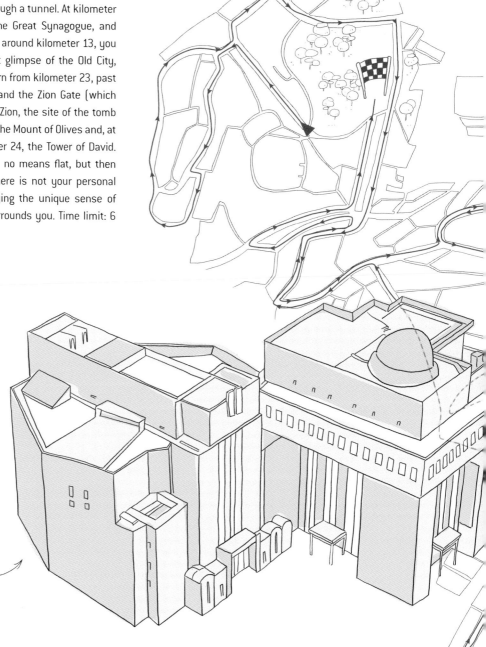

Jerusalem Great Synagogue

Old City

Zion Gate

THE GREAT
BEAUTY

A few years ago, a lot of nonsense was talked about "emotional doping," with people claiming that listening to loud music on your headphones is contrary to the spirit of competitive running and alters your perception. In truth, the case against headphones was also based on safety issues, a much more acceptable argument. Having said that, let me ask a provocative question. If listening to music is "emotional doping," then what about running in races where the scenery is stunning, like along the route from Pallanza to Stresa? Because one thing is certain: the stretch of Lake Maggiore where this half marathon is run is so beautiful that everything else is forgotten, and the colors of nature more than make up for any sense of tiredness or pain. This is what happens when the natural backdrop is so amazing that the race attracts runners from all over the world—in 2014 over 2,300 people made the trip, including the Chinese women's half-marathon squad.

Opposite:
In the second half of the course there are fine views of two of the three Borromean Islands: Isola Superiore and Isola Bella, on which there is a splendid palazzo whose guests included Napoleon.

On pages 48–49:
Verbania Pallanza, where the race starts. The finish is at Stresa on the opposite shore.

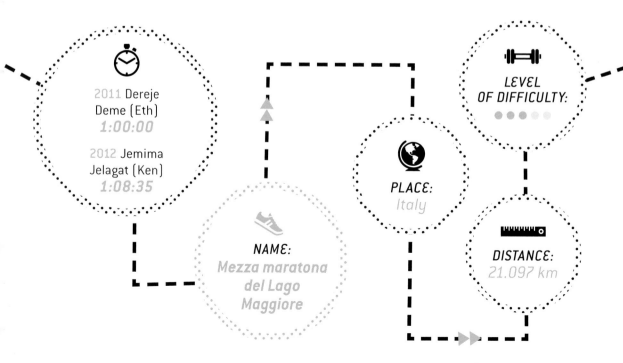

2011 Dereje Deme (Eth)
1:00:00

2012 Jemima Jelagat (Ken)
1:08:35

NAME:
Mezza maratona del Lago Maggiore

PLACE:
Italy

LEVEL OF DIFFICULTY:

DISTANCE:
21.097 km

The race starts on the lakeside in Verbania Pallanza and finishes on the lakeside in Stresa. Compared to the past, the course has been altered slightly—the initial stretch around Villa Taranto has been eliminated, and the stretch near Feriolo has been changed. Once you reach the other shore, you pass through Baveno, where you meet the first of the two climbs at around kilometer 10 (the other one is between kilometers 13 and 14), and finally Stresa. Along the panoramic route between the two resorts, on your left you can admire two of the three Borromean Islands: Isola Superiore and Isola Bella. The race is still not over, however. The changes to the initial stretch have cut out several kilometers, so to make up for this the course continues for around three kilometers beyond Stresa, as far as Belgirate, and then turns back toward the finish. On race day a free boat service ferries runners and spectators between the two resorts. Time limit: 3 hours.

----

1. Lakeside

2. Isola Superiore (or Isola dei Pescatori)

3. Isola Bella

4. Stresa

Lakeside

Isola Bella

A RACE
WITH
ATLANTIC VIEWS

There are cities that seem to have slept deeply for centuries, and others, like Lisbon, whose rich past is immediately apparent. It is impossible to walk around the streets without feeling all the weight of the city's long, intense history, periods of occupation and foreign rule, conquests, art and trade. Lisbon is many things together, a mixed soul, half Mediterranean and half with its gaze directed toward distant routes and far-off continents. Strolling under the porticos of the Café Martinho da Arcada—the oldest in the city, in Praça do Comercio—the atmosphere is so authentic that you get the feeling you might almost bump into the poet Fernando Pessoa, who frequented the café in the early 20th century. The elegant buildings in the center, rebuilt immediately after the devastating earthquake of 1775, form grid-shaped quarters reminiscent, although the architecture is very different, of the blocks of Manhattan. If we were not thousands of miles away, if this were not Europe. But then, as you wait for the cannon shot that gets the race under way on the 25 de Abril Bridge, you can't help thinking of Verrazzano Bridge, and you realize that border territories are all a bit alike. And that you would always like to run in this mild sunshine.

Opposite:
The statue of Christ the King, 28 meters tall, standing on a pedestal 75 meters in height, is clearly inspired by the Christ the Redeemer statue in Rio de Janeiro.

On pages 54–55:
The awe-inspiring start on the 25 de Abril bridge, on the Tagus estuary, renamed in the 1970s to commemorate the Carnation Revolution.

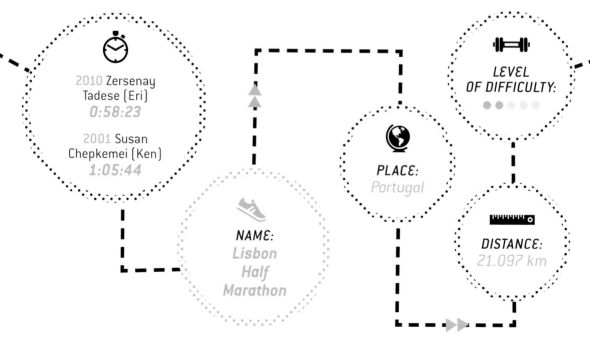

2010 Zersenay Tadese (Eri)
0:58:23

2001 Susan Chepkemei (Ken)
1:05:44

NAME:
*Lisbon
Half
Marathon*

PLACE:
Portugal

LEVEL OF DIFFICULTY:
● ● ○ ○ ○

DISTANCE:
21.097 km

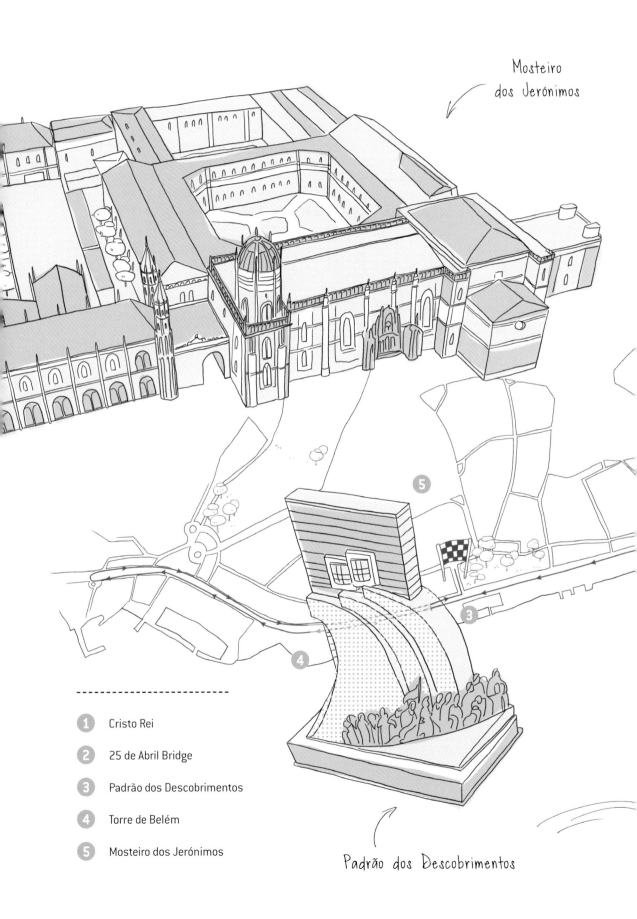

Mosteiro
dos Jerónimos

Padrão dos Descobrimentos

1 Cristo Rei

2 25 de Abril Bridge

3 Padrão dos Descobrimentos

4 Torre de Belém

5 Mosteiro dos Jerónimos

The Lisbon Half Marathon course is flat and straight, which makes it ideal for runners looking for a fast time. The race starts at around 10.30 am from the 25 de Abril Bridge, a great opportunity to enjoy the spectacular view of the city seen from the River Tagus. It then passes through the Alcântara area heading toward the center, as far as the imposing Praça do Comercio, and continues along Avenida 24 de Julho toward Cais do Sodré, where it turns back along the Tagus. From this point on it takes you past some of the city's main sights: from the Padrão dos Descobrimentos, which celebrates the age of the discoveries made by Portuguese navigators, to the famous Torre de Belém, a fortified tower which is now a World Heritage Site. At kilometer 17 is a U-turn and then the final stretch on the way to the finish opposite the Jerónimos Monastery, another place with a long and fascinating history.

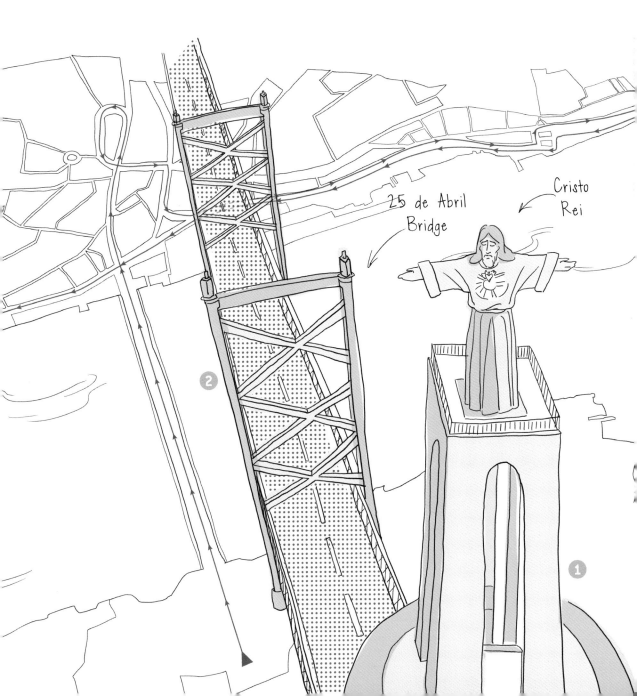

25 de Abril Bridge

Cristo Rei

THE MOST IMPORTANT PART OF A RUNNER'S KIT:
RUNNING SHOES

- -

Another example of technological advances applied to sport is running shoes. The shoes produced by all the main brands are all good quality: what makes the difference is how your feet feel in them. As well as a knowledge of a few fundamental distinctive features.

- -

A QUESTION OF CATEGORY

Running shoes are not all the same, just as runners differ in pace and weight, two essential factors in choosing the right shoes. Nowadays, they are divided into three main categories: A1 (superlight), A2 (intermediate), and A3 (max cushioning), with a difference in weight of around 50 grams, a range that seems fairly insignificant but is actually extremely important. In general, amateur runners opt for shoes with more cushioning (A3), which protects the joints from the damage that can be caused by running for a long time, considering that the majority of runners take three, four, or even five hours to cover the full marathon distance. It's a different story, of course, if you're Kenyan (or in any case a top runner); in this case your skeleto-muscular structure and marathon running speed make superlight shoes more suitable.

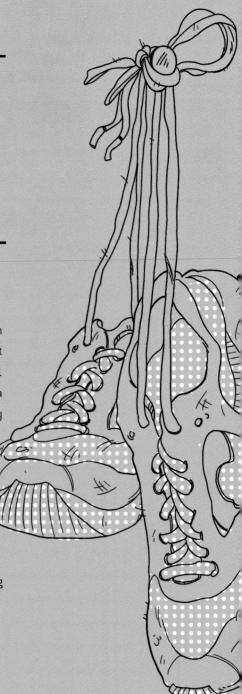

PRONATOR, SUPINATOR, OR NEUTRAL?

Another way of classifying running shoes is on the basis of biomechanics, which often varies from one runner to another. With every stride, you land with a force three times your body weight, which causes your foot to roll slightly to the inside as you strike the ground. Within certain limits, this is a completely natural instinctive movement that allows the body to absorb the shock. In this case it is defined as neutral pronation. An exaggeration of this natural motion is called overpronation, when the foot lands on the outside and then rolls inwards. Supination, on the other hand, is the opposite effect. All the major brands make shoes designed to counter these exaggerated sideways movements.

HOW MANY MILES CAN I DO?

Imagine a motocross bike with badly worn shock absorbers, and the impact this would have on your body at every jolt. This is more or less what happens to your joints and tendons when the midsoles of your running shoes lose their shock-absorption power, generally after 400–500 miles, depending on the model. Usually the wear is accompanied by other visible signs, such as abrasion on the toe cap. So take heed: if you want to avoid injuries keep a record of your mileage, and don't put off buying a new pair of running shoes.

RANDOM TIPS

Let's be honest: most runners have little obsessions that border on the fanatical. For example, even for training runs we insist on double-knotting our laces: nothing annoys us more than having to stop mid-race to tie them up. On the subject of laces, tie them well but not too tight, because your feet tend to swell as you run, forcing you to stop to loosen them. For the same reason, choose running shoes half a size bigger than your normal shoes.

AN ULTRAMARATHON
BETWEEN
TWO OCEANS

What strikes you in South Africa is the light. You think you are familiar with colors, with their various shades and nuances, then you come here and you have to think again. This is not the only surprise, of course. When you stop to chat with the locals, with a taxi-driver or a newspaper vendor, you realize that there this a great sporting tradition in the country, that people are extremely knowledgeable. And we're not just talking about rugby. For example, the Cape Argus, the world's largest timed cycle race, takes place in Cape Town. So it comes as no surprise that running events, like the Two Oceans Marathon, or the equally famous Comrades Marathon, are followed with a passion. This is why, speaking from personal experience, I like to think of South Africa as a vast open-air gym, where you can practice any sport surrounded by breathtaking scenery, from surfing to climbing, from scuba diving to trekking. As well as running, of course.

Opposite:
Chapman's Peak Drive, affectionately known as Chappies, skirts the rocky coastline of Chapman's Peak (593 meters) for 9 kilometers, with a total of 114 bends.

On pages 62–63:
In this part of the world the heat can be a problem, which is why the Two Oceans starts at 6.30 am.

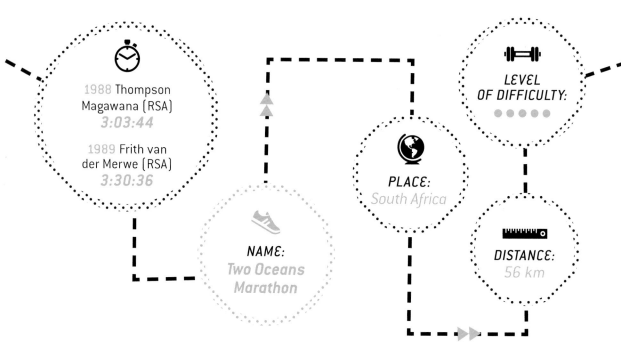

1988 Thompson Magawana (RSA) 3:03:44

1989 Frith van der Merwe (RSA) 3:30:36

NAME:
Two Oceans Marathon

PLACE:
South Africa

LEVEL OF DIFFICULTY:

DISTANCE:
56 km

The Two Oceans is a 56-kilometer ultramarathon which every year attracts over 30,000 runners from all over the world, and is held in Cape Town on Easter Saturday, together with a half marathon and other shorter races. The route is almost circular, starting out at half past six in the morning from Newlands, and finishing at the UCT Rugby Fields. There are "cut-off points" with required times (otherwise you will be asked to retire) at kilometer 25, 38.5, 42, and 46.1. The first part of the course is flat, along the west coast from Muizenberg to Fish Hoek. The race then heads inland across the peninsula, a 10 kilometer stretch (around the half-marathon mark) that links the Atlantic Ocean and the Indian Ocean, which explains the name. Around kilometer 28 you start to climb toward what is one of the toughest, though most scenic, parts of the course: Chapman's Peak Drive, with sheer drops over the sea. When you tackle the climb (and even more so the descent, when you are tempted to run too fast), you should remember to save energy for later, because you're only at kilometer 34 and the finish is still a long way off. When you reach the marathon checkpoint the moment of truth has come—you now have to give it your all, physically and mentally. Another climb, for around four kilometers, first quite gradual, then some short stretches with gradients of up to 10%: welcome to Constantia Nek. Fortunately, from here on in (the last eight kilometers) it's all downhill, with the exception of a few slight slopes. At that point all that remains is to make your triumphant entrance into the sports ground to the cheers of the enthusiastic crowd.

----

1 Kalk Bay

2 Fish Hoek

3 Chapman's Peak Drive

4 Kirstenbosch

Chapman's Peak Drive

Kirstenbosch

④

Kalk Bay

THE IRRESISTIBLE
CHARM OF THE
CÔTE D'AZUR

I ran one of my first half marathons in Nice, and I liked it so much that I went back a couple of years later to run it again. Perhaps it's the French accent, which I find irresistible, or perhaps it's the atmosphere that you soak in as you walk down to the harbor or through the Marché aux Fleurs, lined with restaurants and brasseries—I just love the place. On top of that, the race is really well organized, as usual in France, and the presence of runners from all over Europe gives it a truly international flavor. Another two reasons for entering the race? Going out on Sunday evening to sample the oysters, a local speciality (but remember, don't do this the evening before the race), and the elegant belle époque and Edwardian buildings, which you can admire much better as you run than from a speeding car—and this, as we all know, is one of the joys of running.

Opposite:
The Hotel Negresco, over 100 years old, is a true architectural gem and a part of the city's history.

On pages 68–69:
Palm trees, sun-kissed beaches and blue sea: the Promenade des Anglais, the French Riviera as we imagine it, features in the second half of the race.

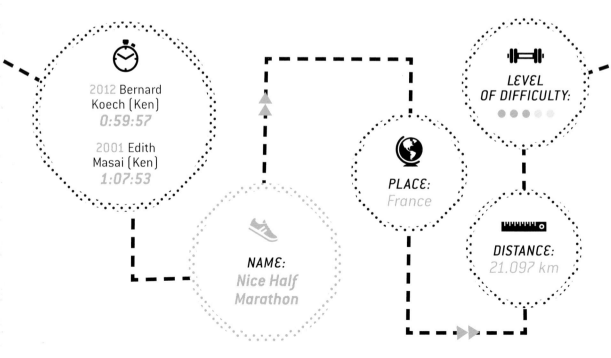

2012 Bernard Koech (Ken)
0:59:57

2001 Edith Masai (Ken)
1:07:53

NAME:
Nice Half Marathon

PLACE:
France

LEVEL OF DIFFICULTY:
● ● ● ○ ○

DISTANCE:
21.097 km

The race starts at 9.30 am from the Promenade des Anglais, opposite the Théâtre de Verdure. The first part of the course goes through the modern city before returning to the harbor and the old city. In the first few kilometers it's a bit congested, and there are also a few short climbs, so you might have to weave in and out a lot. In that case, make sure you don't waste valuable energy—you've got a long way to go to make up for lost time. Along this part of the course you pass the Château de Nice (between kilometers 5 and 6) and then the harbor (at kilometer 8). One tip I would give is this: before you settle in with a group of runners to let them set the pace for you, don't get carried away, because in the first part of the race you'll be surrounded by people running the 10k, and it's likely they'll be going at a pace that's too fast for you. The second part of the course is straight and flat, almost all along the

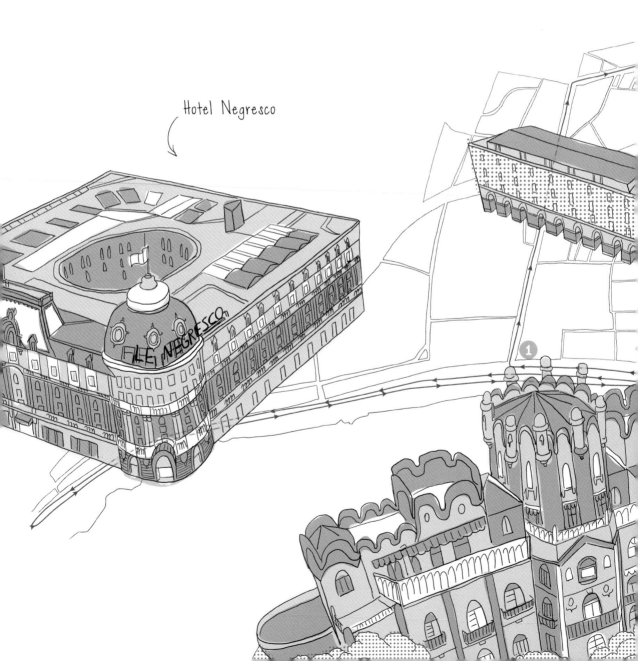

Hotel Negresco

Promenade des Anglais, first toward the international airport and then back after a U-turn toward the finish near the Quai des États-Unis. If it's a sunny day (and this is the Côte d'Azur, after all), in the last few kilometers you'll begin to feel the heat, as well as the mental challenge of a long straight that never seems to end. Keep focused, don't lose heart, and the well-deserved finisher's medal will soon be yours.

1. Hotel Negresco
2. Place Massena
3. Château de Nice
4. Port de Nice

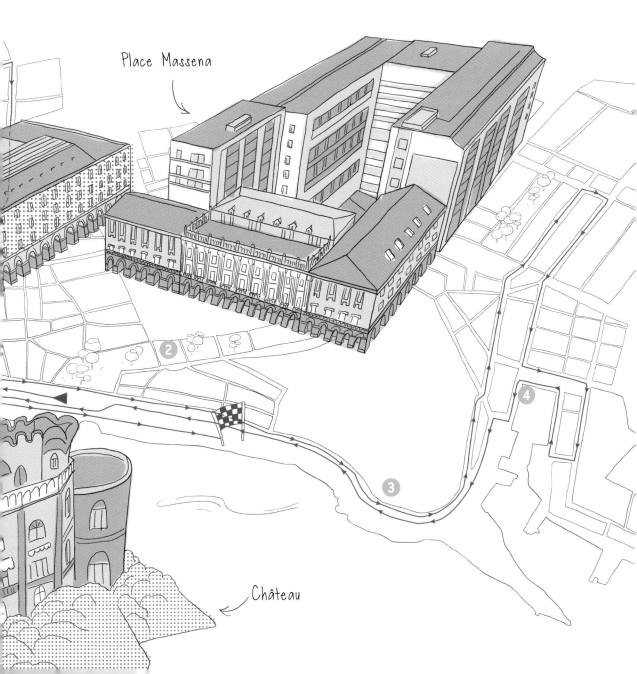

Place Massena

Château

PARIS
IS WELL WORTH
A RUN

Paris has to feature on the list of the five or six "must-do" marathons around the world, for several reasons. The fast, almost completely flat course makes it a good place to run for a personal best. There is so much history and there are so many famous sights along the way that even the most inward-focused runner can't help being captivated. And then there's the impeccable organization and the almost traffic-free roads, even though most of the course takes in the city center. I can assure you that lining up in the start area together with 40,000 marathon runners from 100 or so countries is a thrilling feeling, an experience you only get from major international events. And Paris, which is not a member of the World Marathon Majors only because it does not want to join for political reasons, qualifies as one of the world's genuine top marathons. Run it at least once and you'll love it forever.

Opposite:
The colorful start of the Paris Marathon takes place on the Champs-Elysées. As often happens in big-city marathons, it can take several minutes to cross the starting line.

On pages 74–75:
Straight after the start on the Champs-Elysées the race passes through Place de la Concorde, where the dense throng of runners can slow you down.

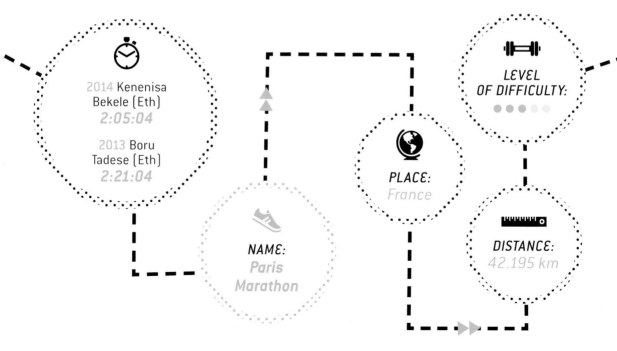

2014 Kenenisa Bekele (Eth)
2:05:04

2013 Boru Tadese (Eth)
2:21:04

NAME:
Paris Marathon

PLACE:
France

LEVEL OF DIFFICULTY:

DISTANCE:
42.195 km

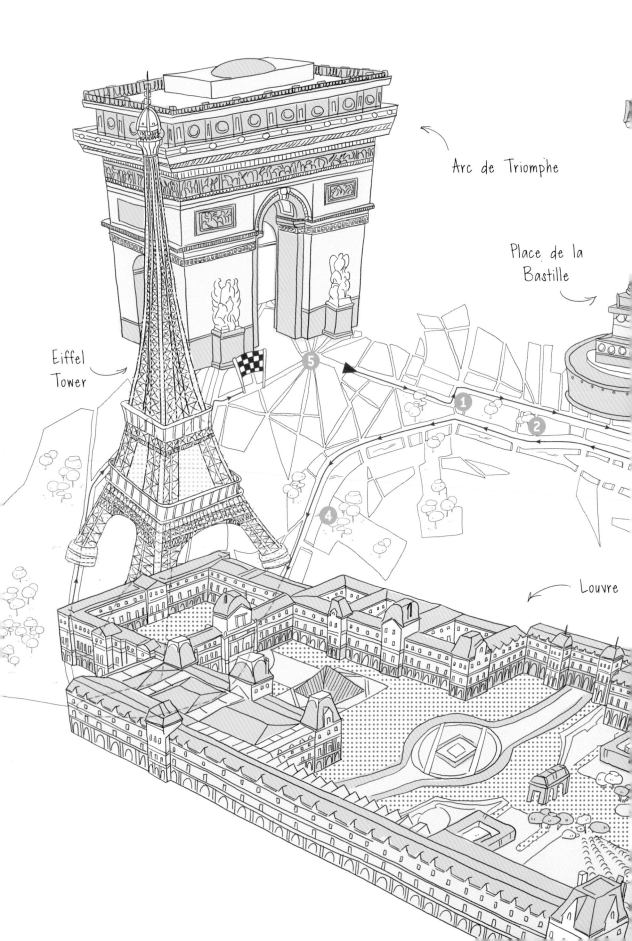

Arc de Triomphe

Place de la Bastille

Eiffel Tower

Louvre

pectacular right from the start, with the colorful river of runners along the tree-lined Champs-Élysées, the race immediately heads past a few of the city's historic landmarks, like the Place de la Concorde, the Place de la Bastille, and the Louvre, before entering the leafy Bois de Vincennes at kilometer 6. The park comes as a welcome relief if you get a hot day (as I did), but it can be tough if it's cold and windy. From kilometer 23 you follow the Seine (with Notre-Dame on your left at kilometer 24), through a series of underpasses that can be quite challenging. You'll be ready for this, of course, after including a few tunnels in your training program! Hardly time to admire the Eiffel Tower at kilometer 29 and you're already in Rue de Mirabeau, where a tough one-kilometer climb awaits you. A quick glimpse of the Parc des Princes stadium on your left and you enter the Bois de Boulogne for your final sprint (well that's the idea, anyway!). The finish is in Avenue Foch near the Arc de Triomphe. Start time 8.45 am. Time limit: 5 hours 40 minutes.

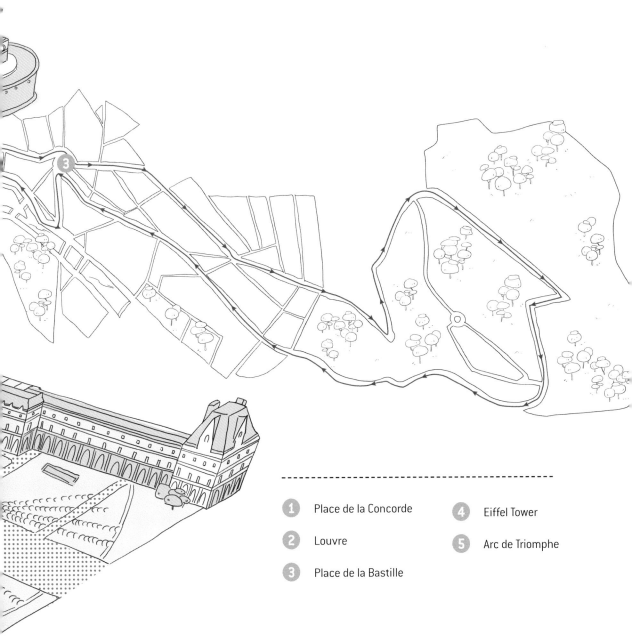

1 Place de la Concorde
2 Louvre
3 Place de la Bastille
4 Eiffel Tower
5 Arc de Triomphe

LONDON
RUNNING

£53 million—this was the astounding sum raised for charity by runners in the 2013 London Marathon. A figure which not only is a world record for funds raised by a single event, but also serves to give the measure of what this race is all about, aside from purely sporting matters, for the international running community: a fantastic collective effort from the 36,000 runners and the innumerable people who give their support to the marathon charities. On the other hand, to quote from the 1988 baseball movie *Bull Durham*, "sometimes it rains," and if you're unlucky, as I was, you might have to run the whole race in a constant downpour. But it's an ill wind that blows no good: without the inclement weather I would never have had the chance to appreciate the great sporting spirit of the London crowds, who lined the course in their thousands, undeterred. They wouldn't have missed the show for anything.

Opposite:
The end of the race on the Mall, where the Royal Family might be watching!

On pages 80–81:
One of the highlights of the course, when the runners cross Tower Bridge, around the halfway mark, with great views of the Thames and the city.

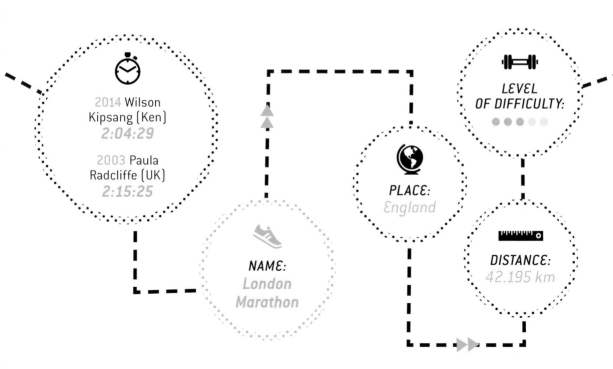

2014 Wilson Kipsang (Ken) *2:04:29*

2003 Paula Radcliffe (UK) *2:15:25*

NAME: *London Marathon*

PLACE: *England*

LEVEL OF DIFFICULTY: ●●●●○

DISTANCE: *42.195 km*

The London Marathon sets out at 10 am from Greenwich Park (which hosts the Prime Meridian Line, in case you'd forgotten!) in the south of the city. In order to avoid congestion, which could hold the faster runners up, there are three start points, based on previous or predicted times, more or less like in New York. The first stretch is slightly downhill, before all the courses join up after 2.8 miles. At mile 6 you pass the Cutty Sark, the historic clipper now open to the public. At about mile 12 you enter the heart of the city, past one of London's great landmarks, Tower Bridge (near which you pass again at mile 22), with a view of the Tower of London, then at mile 19 you reach Canary Wharf, one of London's business districts, with its spectacular skyline, including the famous Millennium Dome. After passing near Tower Bridge for a second time the route takes you along the Thames. Here you come to the Blackfriars underpass, which can be tough, with a climb that you could do without at this point in the race. Fortunately,

London Eye

Houses of Parliament

Tower Bridge

when you emerge the sight of Westminster and Big Ben tells you that you're nearing the end. Just time enough to skirt St. James's Park, wave to the Royal Family and head into the Mall, with huge crowds cheering you on, for the last few meters of a marathon you will never forget. Time limit: 8 hours. The London Marathon is very well organized, and the English think of everything, with volunteers even handing out vaseline to runners to prevent blisters.

1 Tower Bridge

2 Canary Wharf

3 London Eye

4 Houses of Parliament

5 Buckingham Palace

6 The Mall

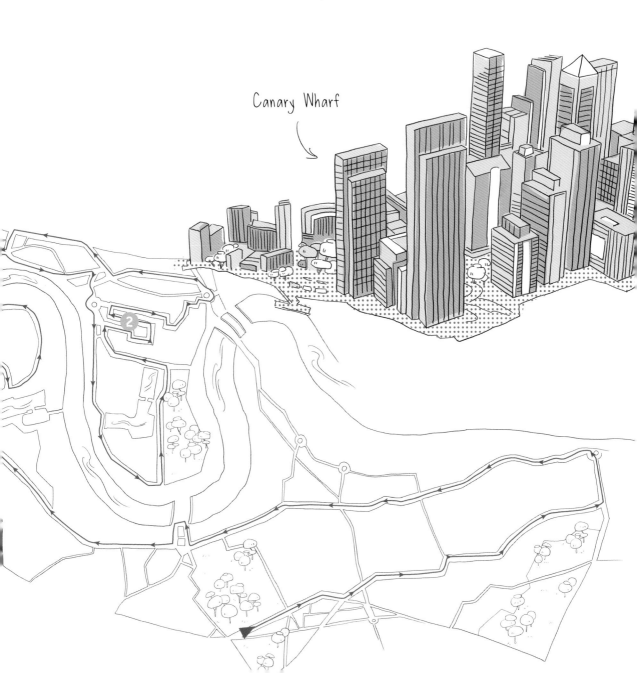

Canary Wharf

THE MOTHER
OF ALL
MARATHONS

The day might come when you look back and realize that you have run lots of races around the world, like a series of flags planted on a world map, proven by the heavy tangle of medals that your wife would like to relegate to the loft. And at that point, like a young boy with his football stickers, "Got, not got," you will feel the urgent need to run the Boston Marathon. Why? Because that's where it all began, in 1897, and because for a 21st-century runner the Boston Marathon is like a pilgrimage to Mecca: you have to go at least once in your life. No marathon is so steeped in history and tradition as this one. And holding it on Patriot's Day, the third Monday in April, makes it as American as you can get. Yet in reality Boston belongs to us all, as we saw the year after the bombings in 2013, when the number of participants shot up to 36,000. A gesture of love for what is a world heritage for runners.

Opposite:
After the bombings in 2013, security at the Boston Marathon has been further increased. The photo shows the finish area on Boylston Street.

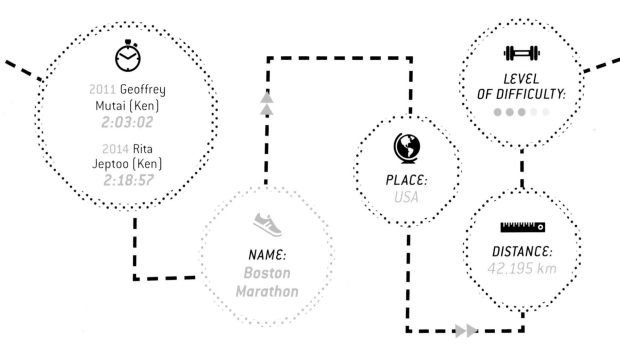

2011 Geoffrey Mutai (Ken)
2:03:02

2014 Rita Jeptoo (Ken)
2:18:57

NAME:
Boston Marathon

PLACE:
USA

LEVEL OF DIFFICULTY:

DISTANCE:
42.195 km

With a staggered "wave start," the race sets out from Hopkinton and heads along Route 135, passing through Ashland, Framingham, and Natick, and is slightly downhill up to the halfway point. Just after the half-marathon mark you come to the Newton Hills, and it is here that the race really starts: around nine miles of hills, culminating between the 20 and 21-mile marks, near Boston College, with the famous Heartbreak Hill. It owes its name to an episode that took place in 1936, when John Kelley overtook Ellison Brown, giving him a consolatory pat on the shoulder as he passed. Brown, understandably furious, rallied and took the lead again, winning the race and—in the words of a *Globe* reporter—breaking Kelley's heart. If you don't want your heart to break, tackle the four hills one by one in your mind: when you've done one, put it behind you and concentrate on the next. Believe me, it works. Another tip: there'll be around a million spectators cheering you on around the course. This is fantastic, of course, but don't waste too much energy giving high fives. The other important thing to know is that you can only register if you have achieved the qualifying times, which vary according to age, in the previous 18 months. Time limit: 6 hours 30 minutes.

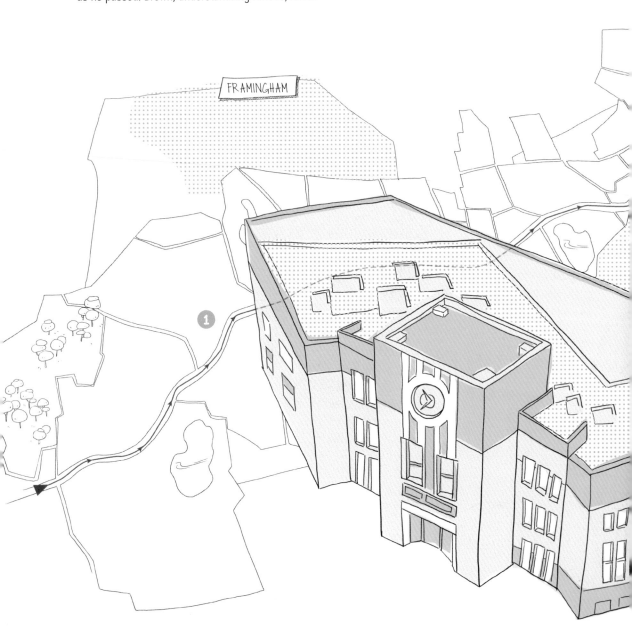

FRAMINGHAM

1

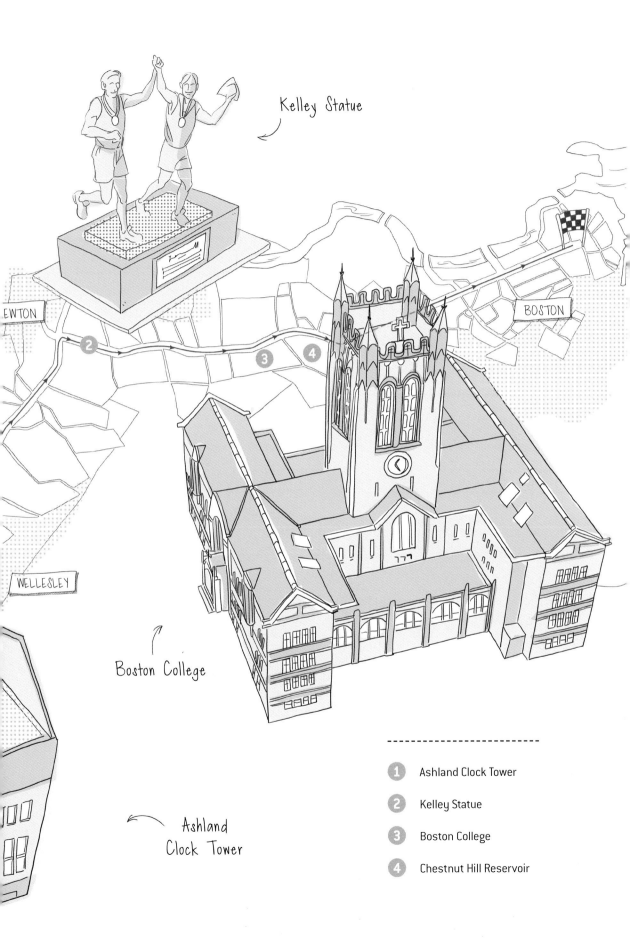

Kelley Statue

EWTON

BOSTON

WELLESLEY

Boston College

Ashland
Clock Tower

1 Ashland Clock Tower

2 Kelley Statue

3 Boston College

4 Chestnut Hill Reservoir

Runners passing the First Congregational Church in Natick, at around mile 9. The town of Natick, about 10 miles from Boston, was the site of the first baseball factory in the United States, founded in 1858.

A picture from the 2009 Boston Marathon, showing the leading group that contained the first three runners home: the Ethiopian Deriba Merga, the Kenyan Daniel Rono (partly hidden in a yellow vest) and the American Ryan Hall.

THE PIANIST
ON THE OCEAN

Big Sur is a region of the Central Coast of California, a region of stunning natural beauty with mountains and sheer drops to the sea, imposing giant redwoods and beautiful cacti. A wild landscape, far from the palms of Beverly Hills or the beaches of Malibu. The idea of running a marathon here—an idea which first came to founder Bill Burleigh in the mid-1980s—is both a challenge and an unmissable opportunity to run in a unique setting. Along Highway 101, in fact, around every bend there is another spectacular view of the ocean. So for once you should leave your competitive instincts and your stopwatch at home, relax, enjoy the views, and maybe take a few photos. To be at the start on time you'll probably have to get up at three in the morning, but who cares when you can have your photo taken with a tuxedo-clad piano player halfway across a bridge over the ocean?

Opposite:
Highway 101, with its stunning views over the wildest cliffs in California.

On pages 92–93:
One of the highlights of the race: Bixby Bridge, where a tuxedo-clad pianist awaits the runners.

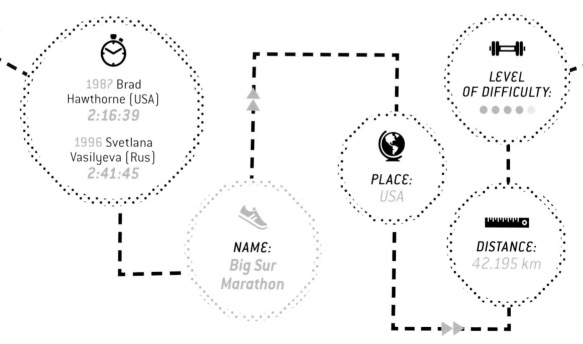

1987 Brad Hawthorne (USA)
2:16:39

1996 Svetlana Vasilyeva (Rus)
2:41:45

LEVEL OF DIFFICULTY:
● ● ● ● ○

PLACE:
USA

NAME:
Big Sur Marathon

DISTANCE:
42.195 km

The first adversary to beat in a marathon like the Big Sur is the heat. Which is why the race starts at 6.45 am (with three waves a few minutes apart). The start is at Big Sur Station, 90 meters above sea level. Up to mile 5 the course is slightly downhill, then it climbs toward Point Sur, where there is a fantastic view of the Pacific Ocean with the picturesque lighthouse on the promontory and the Pico Blanco on your right. Don't let yourself get distracted, however, and save your energy, because mile 10 marks the beginning of the ascent to Hurricane Point, a 160-meter climb in around two miles: this is the toughest part of the course, just focus on taking one step at a time without thinking too much. At the summit you start to descend toward the famed Bixby Bridge, where there are often strong gusts of wind, another feature of the race not to be underestimated. Before you rugged scenery, waves beating

Bixby Bridge

CARMEL

Pico Blanco

against the rocks, and, if you're lucky, sea lions as spectators. If you think you can hear piano music in the distance, don't put it down to tiredness or the wind. It's actually a real pianist, playing his grand piano to accompany you as you cross the bridge—a genuinely moving moment for anyone with a sensitive soul. From now on the course is undulating all the way to the finish at Rio Road. Time limit: 6 hours.

1 Point Sur

2 Hurricane Point

3 Pico Blanco

4 Bixby Bridge

Hurricane Point

TRAINING

Running seems simple enough: you just lace up your shoes and go. But when you decide you'd like to improve and start looking at training plans, you're likely to come across such an overwhelming amount of information, new terms, programs, and advice that it's easy to get confused. So how should you get started?

FROM JOGGER TO RUNNER

The ability to run for at least an hour can be considered the dividing line between running just to keep fit and serious running. It is the minimum requirement to plan a training program that will gradually allow you (and "gradually" is the key word here) to tackle longer distances: from 10k to the half marathon, right up to the ultimate goal, the marathon, the most testing distance, which for this reason should be approached with due caution. First of all, you should get a medical certificate proving you are fit to run, a requirement in some countries if you want to compete in races. After which, be patient and don't do too much too soon. If you're new to running, start with 20–30 minutes, two or three times a week, at a pace that allows you to converse easily (the so-called "talk test"), building up in the space of a few weeks to 40–50 minutes, with the last 10 minutes at a slightly faster pace.

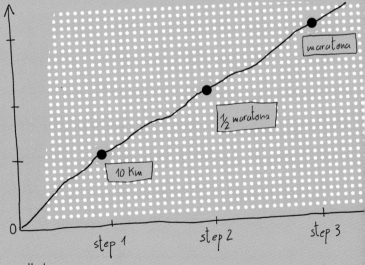

SOLO OR IN A GROUP?

For some people running is a meditative experience that requires perfect solitude. Other people prefer the social side of running. Running with others can be fun, but be careful when you're training with more experienced runners, because you might be tempted go beyond your own limits. Never push yourself too hard, especially at the beginning, to keep up with a faster runner. Running with others, especially if you're a beginner, you'll get lots of advice—often contradictory—on every aspect of running, from how many times a week you should train to whether or not you should use sports supplements, whether it's better to run in the morning on an empty stomach, and so on and so forth. Listen to everyone, but most importantly listen to yourself, and try out some of the tips, perhaps adapting them to your own needs.

CROSS-TRAINING

Don't be obsessive and don't make the mistake of overdoing the running. Rest is an essential part of any athlete's training. And now and then it's a good idea to include other activities like swimming or biking in your training schedule: as well as adding variety, this will help you to strengthen muscle groups that are used less in running. And remember, stretching is essential to relax the muscles and prevent injuries, just as you should always devote a few minutes a week to exercises designed to strengthen your core, the abdominal muscles that help you to improve balance and stability.

THE VARIOUS TYPES OF TRAINING RUN

This is not a running handbook, so I won't go into too much technical detail here. But generally speaking, it's enough to know that running at specific paces brings about the physiological changes that allow you to improve your performance and, for example, to complete your first marathon. This is exactly the logic behind the cryptic terms typical of runners' slang—"long runs," "fartlek," "tempo runs," "aerobic threshold," and so on: developing the body's capacity to improve consumption and performance, teaching it to improve the supply of oxygen to the muscles, to burn fat (and not only glycogen), to reduce lactic acid build-up, and so on. One last word of advice: in specialized magazines and on websites you'll find lots of ready-made training schedules. Always bear in mind that these are inevitably one-size-fits-all, and should be tailored to your own needs.

A JOURNEY
IN THE HEART
OF ITALY

This is not a race in the strict sense of the term, although the results are published, and there is a winner. Italy Coast to Coast is more like a journey, when what counts is looking around yourself, and perhaps into yourself. Due to the limited number of competitors (inevitable in a 300 kilometer race with hundreds of junctions, crossroads, and roundabouts), a friendly spirit is soon established, and it's a bit like a convoy of friends crossing Italy from coast to coast, over hills, along country paths, and up mountains. And setting up camp every evening near some of Italy's artistic and architectural treasures, like tiny hamlets or medieval abbeys. A shared adventure made up of a lot of effort (it is a run, after all, and a long run at that), but also contemplation and high spirits, joking and good food. A dream to be lived, though only if you forget your stopwatch and enjoy all the silence and beauty of one of the loveliest parts of Italy. And all without ever meeting traffic lights.

Opposite:
A view of Mount Amiata from the Val d'Orcia, part of the third stage of the race. The route takes in a wide variety of geographical areas, with very different weather conditions. It's not unusual to experience baking sun, sudden storms and low temperatures all on the same day.

On pages 100–101:
Surrounded by vineyards, nestling on a sun-drenched hill, the Castle of Poggio alle Mura, near Montalcino, is one of the beautiful views that runners can admire during the fourth stage. But then in the Italy Coast to Coast contemplation and enjoyment of the natural surroundings are an essential part of the whole race experience.

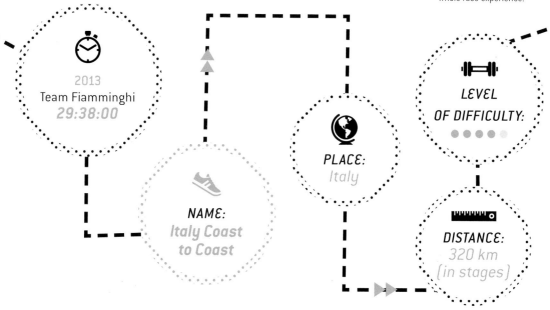

2013
Team Fiamminghi
29:38:00

NAME:
Italy Coast to Coast

PLACE:
Italy

LEVEL OF DIFFICULTY:
●●●●○

DISTANCE:
320 km (in stages)

taly Coast to Coast is a relay race for teams of four runners. Almost 320 kilometers in four stages, from the Adriatic Sea to the Tyrrhenian Sea, with overnight stops like in cycling races. The first stage (85 kilometers) is from the medieval hamlet of Montedinove to the Abbey of Sant'Eutizio, leading inland through the Marche, crossing the Monti Sibillini and entering Umbria. Here you reach an altitude of 1,742 meters, the highest point in the whole race. The second stage (84 kilometers) takes you across the Foligno plain and through the Tiber Valley, along a stretch of the Via Francigena, where the toughest challenge is the change from the cool temperatures on the high ground to the humidity and traffic around the built-up areas, always skirted on secondary roads. The third stage (88 kilometers), halfway between the two seas, brings you into Tuscany, where undulating paths take you across the Val d'Orcia before you head toward Monte Amiata. The final stage (60 kilometers), through extremely varied scenery, starts out from the beautiful Abbey of Sant'Antimo and continues through the vineyards of Brunello di Montalcino as far as the castle of Poggio alle Mura, before heading into the heart of the Maremma region. After a long section along woodland paths, you finally reach the splendid inlet of Cala Violina, where a quick swim is the best way to celebrate your achievement. As well as signs all along the course, the organizers also provide a roadbook, assistance, (very creative) refreshment stations, and a transport service to cut out short sections that are either monotonous or traffic-congested.

----

1   Monti Sibillini

2   Castle of Poggio alle Mura

3   Abbey of Sant'Antimo

4   Cala Violina

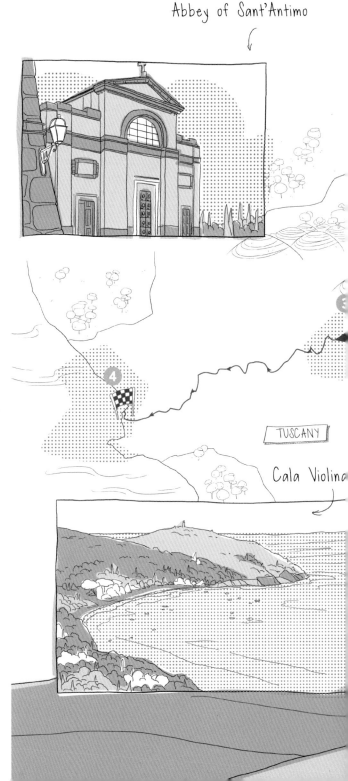

Abbey of Sant'Antimo

TUSCANY

Cala Violina

Castle of Poggio alle Mura

MARCHE

UMBRIA

Monti Sibillini

THE TRUE
SPIRIT OF
SAN FRANCISCO

At 5.13 am on 18 April 1906 a devastating earthquake followed by uncontrol-lable fires destroyed San Francisco. Among the events that followed the initial reconstruction, some aimed to lift the city's spirits. One of these was a 12-kilo-meters footrace that crossed the city from the Bay area to the Great Highway, in front of the Pacific Coast's Ocean Beach. First run in 1912, the race is now known as San Francisco's Bay to Breakers. Over a hundred years have gone by since then, but the colorful race has maintained its original spirit: a real cel-ebration with a party atmosphere, much loved by the locals but also attended by runners from further afield. A race where what counts is not competition but the desire to celebrate the unique energy of a city that never stops mov-ing. With an astonishing 110,000 participants, the Bay to Breakers race held in 1986 was recognized by the Guinness Book of World Records as the world's largest footrace.

Opposite:
Few races manage to attract a mix of serious runners and runners who just want to have fun like the Bay to Breakers, one of the oldest and most colorful running events in the world.

On pages 106–107:
The so-called "painted ladies," colorful Victorian buildings, seen from Alamo Square Park, one of the most interesting and picturesque areas in the city.

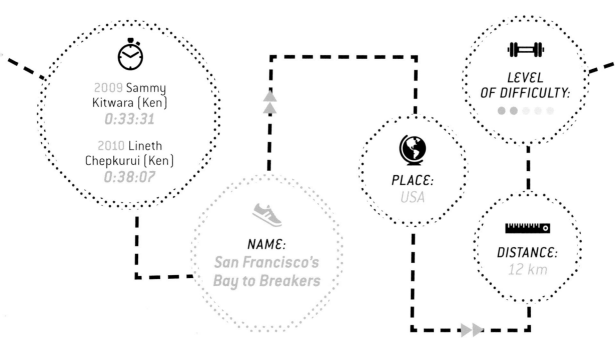

2009 Sammy Kitwara (Ken)
0:33:31

2010 Lineth Chepkurui (Ken)
0:38:07

LEVEL OF DIFFICULTY:
● ● ○ ○ ○

PLACE:
USA

NAME:
San Francisco's Bay to Breakers

DISTANCE:
12 km

A FESTIVAL
OF
RUNNING

I'm not sure, but I imagine that when foreigners associate Scotland with whisky, kilts, and bagpipes it is as annoying for the Scottish as it is for the Italians to hear Italy talked about in terms of pizza, spaghetti, and mandolino. Unfortunately, stereotypes never go away. But I love the Scots, because they have a powerful sense of tradition, they're a bit crazy, and they're extremely sociable, especially after a few beers. During the Edinburgh Marathon Festival weekend, which includes a half marathon and several shorter races, the locals take to the streets and cheer everyone on enthusiastically, just as you would expect from the passionate Scots. As you run you can't help admiring the city's natural elegance, and it comes as no surprise that with its rich architectural heritage it has been recognized as a World Heritage Site.

Opposite:
View of Edinburgh with Arthur's Seat, an unusual geological formation that offers a great view of the city, in the background.

On pages 112–113:
During the first few miles runners pass the Scottish Parliament Building and one of the royal residences in Holyrood Park.

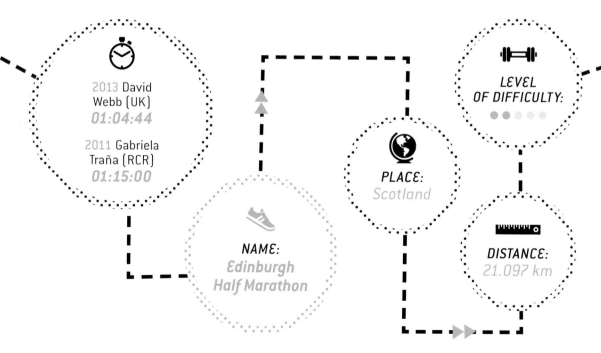

2013 David Webb (UK) *01:04:44*

2011 Gabriela Traña (RCR) *01:15:00*

NAME:
Edinburgh Half Marathon

PLACE:
Scotland

LEVEL OF DIFFICULTY:

DISTANCE:
21.097 km

The course is flat—great if you are looking for a personal best or if it's your first half marathon. Following part of the marathon route, the race sets off from Regent Road and then crosses Holyrood Park, which hosts one of the Queen's official residences. From here you get a great view of Arthur's Seat, a rocky peak formed by an extinct volcano. Between mile 3 and mile 4 you come to Leith Links, the site of important historical events such as the Siege of Leith. From mile 5 the race follows the seafront along Portobello Promenade, then cuts slightly inland onto Musselburgh Road. At the eight mile mark you pass close to the finish, but first you have five miles out and back along Ravensheugh Road. The finish is at Musselburgh Racecourse. Time limit: 3 hours.

1 Regent Road

2 Portobello Promenade

3 Musselburgh Racecourse

4 Holyrood Park

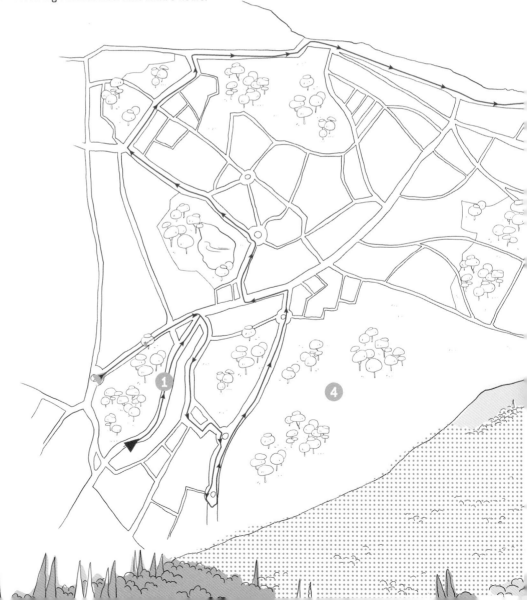

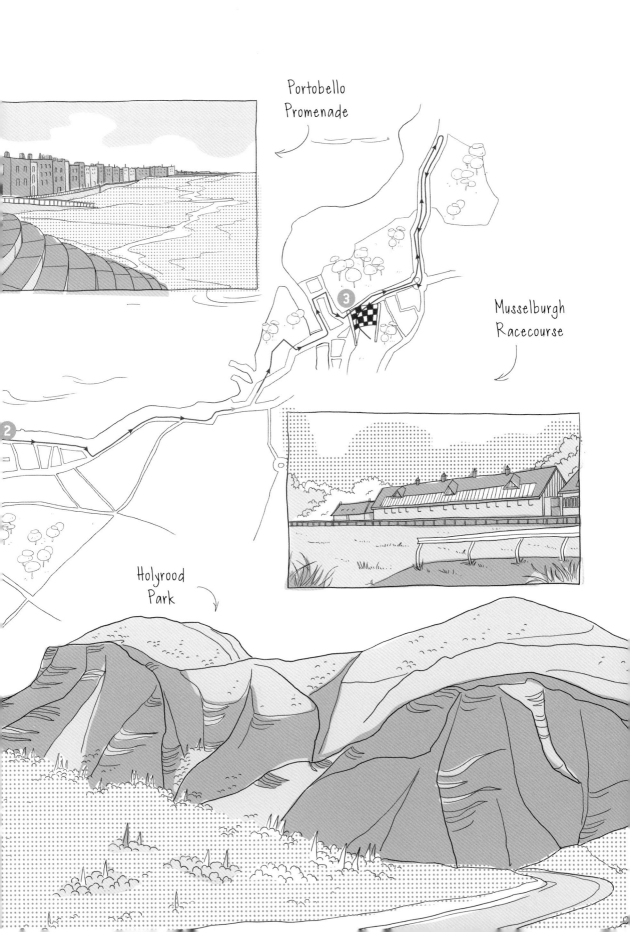

Portobello
Promenade

Musselburgh
Racecourse

Holyrood
Park

NUTRITION AND HYDRATION

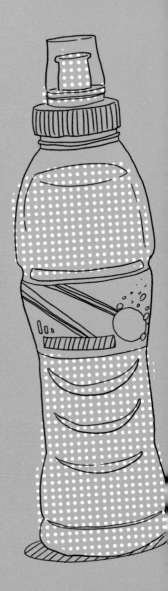

What should you eat before a workout? And after? Sooner or later runners start to pay more attention to food and drink, partly because running tends naturally to become part of a healthy lifestyle (also from a nutritional point of view), and partly because we realize that quality "fuel" improves performance. So what is the secret of good nutrition? Don't go to extremes, don't deprive your body of macronutrients, and don't skip meals. On the contrary, eat often and in a balanced manner, remembering that the needs of a runner, in terms of both quantity and quality, are different from those of people who don't practice any sport.

FOOD AND RUNNING

On this subject there are no formulas that suit everyone. However, from certain common dietary errors it is possible to draw a few general conclusions. It is a mistake, for example, to increase substantially the amount of high-glycemic carbohydrates you consume. It is true that bread and pasta are an essential source of "fuel" for an athlete's muscles (so it would be wrong to cut them out altogether), but if you are not a professional athlete your daily intake should be kept within reasonable limits. Another mistake is to skip meals, for various reasons: first of all, because instead of allowing you to lose weight this causes a reduction in lean mass (muscles); and then because the consequent increase in glucose—which raises the level of insulin in the blood—accelerates the conversion of fat into sugar the next time you eat, bringing about the opposite effect. It is much more sensible to eat snacks during the day, and in general to cut down on bread, pasta, potatoes, meat, and dairy foods, in favor of low-glycemic carbohydrates, such as fiber-rich vegetables, which strengthen lean body mass. Chicken, turkey, and fish are good sources of protein. It is also important to cut down on alcohol and sugar (which can be replaced by honey or fructose), and to use extra-virgin olive oil rather than butter. Your normal food intake will suffice to replace lost fluids and energy after a normal workout, but after intense physical exertion (like a marathon) the animal proteins contained in meat will help to repair micro-tears in the muscle tissue.

NUTRITION TIPS

In general you should eat at least three to four hours before a workout. If you're planning to do a long run and you don't want to run out of energy, eat a healthy breakfast, including toast, jam, or honey, but avoiding milk and yogurt, which are more difficult to digest. For workouts of up to 60 minutes, some people prefer not to eat at all; this is a personal choice, usually to prevent stomach problems or to avoid having to get up too early. This is fine, but only—as I said—for less demanding workouts. Another important tip: in the last few days before a race, don't alter your eating habits. At most, before a marathon you can vary the proportions of the various nutrients, eating more high-carb foods (though without overdoing it), backing off on fat and protein, and limiting high-fiber foods.

RUNNING IN THE HEAT

In very hot weather, much of the energy produced when running is dispersed through sweat. A complex mechanism activates perspiration, causing dehydration which, if neglected, affects your performance and subjects the organism to a degree of stress that often leads to cramp or, even worse, heatstroke. This explains the importance of drinking before you feel thirsty—even before you begin physical exercise—and of continuing to drink during and after your run, in order to replace lost fluids. It can also be a good idea to train early in the morning, when the temperature is lower, or perhaps to use a treadmill.

SUPPLEMENTS

Supplements such as energy bars, protein bars, gels, and maltodextrin can be a precious ally. For example, when the weather is hot an isotonic drink before and during a run or an instant drink for quick recovery will allow you to replace lost salts and fluids quickly and efficiently. Only don't overdo it, and don't make the mistake of thinking that supplements can make up for lack of training. In other words, don't kid yourself that they'll do all the work even if you haven't trained properly. Finally, make sure you test each variety during training runs: you don't want an upset stomach during a race!

THROUGH
THE DOLOMITES

Forget the glossy, upmarket image of Cortina d'Ampezzo that you see in films, magazines and Christmas TV programs. Or rather, try to put it to the back of your mind, because it is actually very close to the truth. The race sets out from the center of the capital of the Dolomites, but fortunately it's early and the shops are still closed. After just a few kilometers you're running on trails used by cross-country skiers in the winter and mountain bikers in the summer, along a disused railway line through the heart of the Dolomites. The first part of the race is all uphill, a constant, though fairly gentle, climb, across wooden bridges or through cool, picturesque tunnels, which as well as being very atmospheric is also a relief on a hot June morning. Once you reach the top and pass the Lake of Landro, the path downhill is slightly more uneven, but this is more than made up for by the stunning view on your right of the Three Peaks of Lavaredo. From kilometer 20 you continue to pick up speed as you go downhill, right up to Lake Dobbiaco, the park, and the baskets of apples at the finish. A different race, and an unusual distance, so it's impossible to compare your time with previous races. Which makes it all the more enjoyable.

Opposite:
One of the highlights of the Cortina–Dobbiaco, when the race passes through one of the two tunnels along the disused railway line that ran from Calalzo to Dobbiaco until the 1960s.

On pages 120–121:
What makes the Cortina–Dobbiaco unique is the stunning Dolomite scenery along the route. Slightly uphill for the first 14 kilometers, the course then descends gradually to the finish.

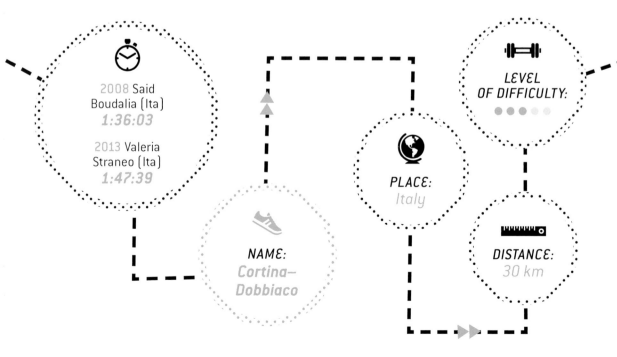

2008 Said Boudalia (Ita)
1:36:03

2013 Valeria Straneo (Ita)
1:47:39

NAME:
Cortina–Dobbiaco

PLACE:
Italy

LEVEL OF DIFFICULTY:

DISTANCE:
30 km

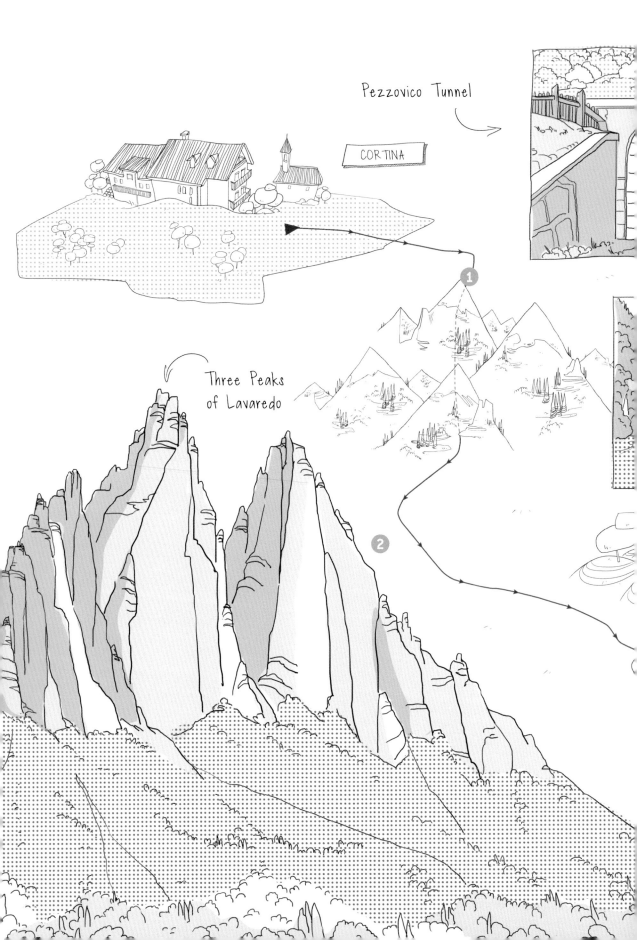

Pezzovico Tunnel

CORTINA

Three Peaks
of Lavaredo

1

2

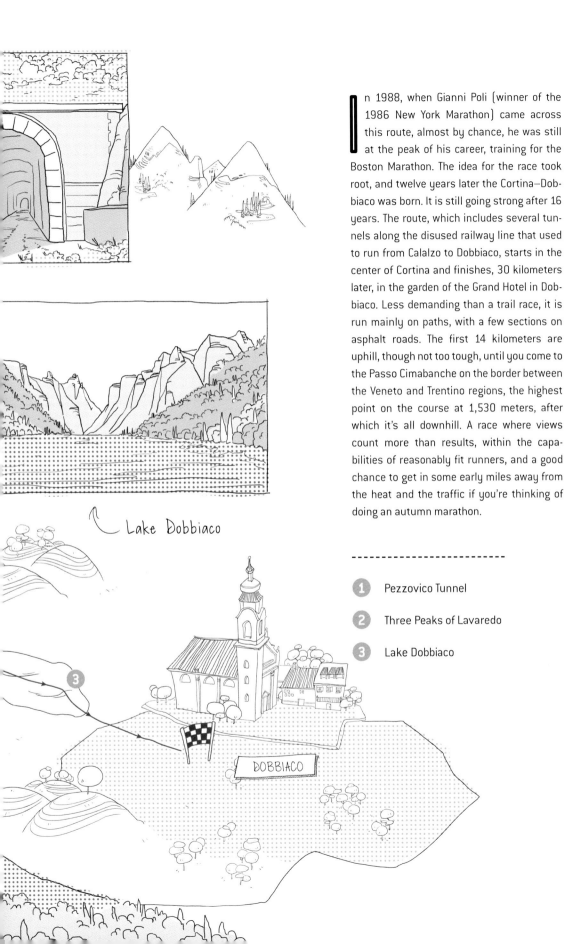

Lake Dobbiaco

I n 1988, when Gianni Poli (winner of the 1986 New York Marathon) came across this route, almost by chance, he was still at the peak of his career, training for the Boston Marathon. The idea for the race took root, and twelve years later the Cortina–Dobbiaco was born. It is still going strong after 16 years. The route, which includes several tunnels along the disused railway line that used to run from Calalzo to Dobbiaco, starts in the center of Cortina and finishes, 30 kilometers later, in the garden of the Grand Hotel in Dobbiaco. Less demanding than a trail race, it is run mainly on paths, with a few sections on asphalt roads. The first 14 kilometers are uphill, though not too tough, until you come to the Passo Cimabanche on the border between the Veneto and Trentino regions, the highest point on the course at 1,530 meters, after which it's all downhill. A race where views count more than results, within the capabilities of reasonably fit runners, and a good chance to get in some early miles away from the heat and the traffic if you're thinking of doing an autumn marathon.

----

1 Pezzovico Tunnel

2 Three Peaks of Lavaredo

3 Lake Dobbiaco

DOBBIACO

IMPERIAL
PROSPECT

Until the fall of the Berlin Wall, what little I knew about the Russia came from spy novels and movies. From their language to their customs, almost everything about this people, actually not that far away from us in geographical terms, seemed (and to some extent still seems) mysterious, and therefore fascinating, in some ways even more interesting than America. And if it is true that running in a city is an excellent way of getting to know the local culture, then running in St. Petersburg, the city founded by Peter the Great, the seat of the court of the tsars, which with its many islands is slightly reminiscent of Venice, is an opportunity to immerse yourself in its art, history, and culture. Add to that the fact that the St. Petersburg 10k is run during the "White Nights," a phenomenon that takes place during the summer solstice, when the sun never drops below the horizon. To celebrate the season of the midnight sun, every year the city organizes a festival with ballet, opera, and music events that make the atmosphere even more magical.

Opposite:
The Church of the Savior on Spilled Blood, one of the most important Orthodox churches in the city. It was built on the site where Tsar Alexander II was assassinated and was dedicated to his memory.

On pages 126–127:
When the race takes place the city welcomes visitors with the many concerts and other events of the "White Nights" festival, held during the summer solstice.

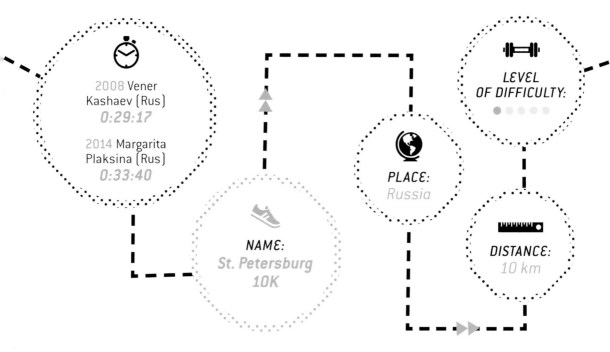

2008 Vener Kashaev (Rus)
0:29:17

2014 Margarita Plaksina (Rus)
0:33:40

NAME:
St. Petersburg 10K

PLACE:
Russia

LEVEL OF DIFFICULTY:
● ○ ○ ○ ○

DISTANCE:
10 km

distance any runner can handle and a beautiful course through the city: two good reasons for taking part in this 10-kilometer race. The start is in Palace Square, close to Nevsky Prospect, the main road that crosses the city, near the Church of the Savior. In front of you, on the banks of the Neva, a series of famous landmarks will leave you breathless: the Hermitage Museum, the Winter Palace, the Admiralty building and St. Isaac's Cathedral with its gilded dome. And this is all in the first kilometer! The race then continues along the other bank of the Neva, before turning left. At kilometer 5 is another bridge, and a section along the opposite bank toward the Peter and Paul Fortress, built in 1703 by Peter the Great, where Dostoevsky, among others, was imprisoned and very nearly executed. Hardly time to take everything in and you're already crossing Trinity Bridge, which brings you back to the mainland, where you pass another architectural jewel, the Marble Palace, before reaching the finish.

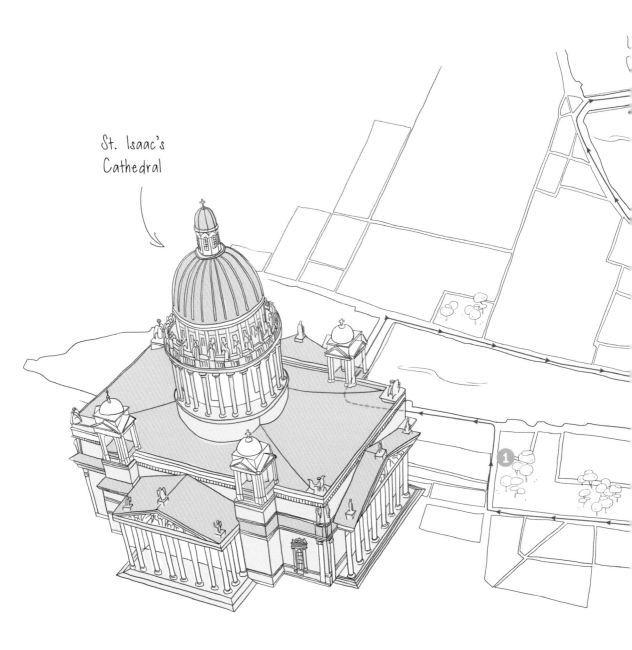

St. Isaac's Cathedral

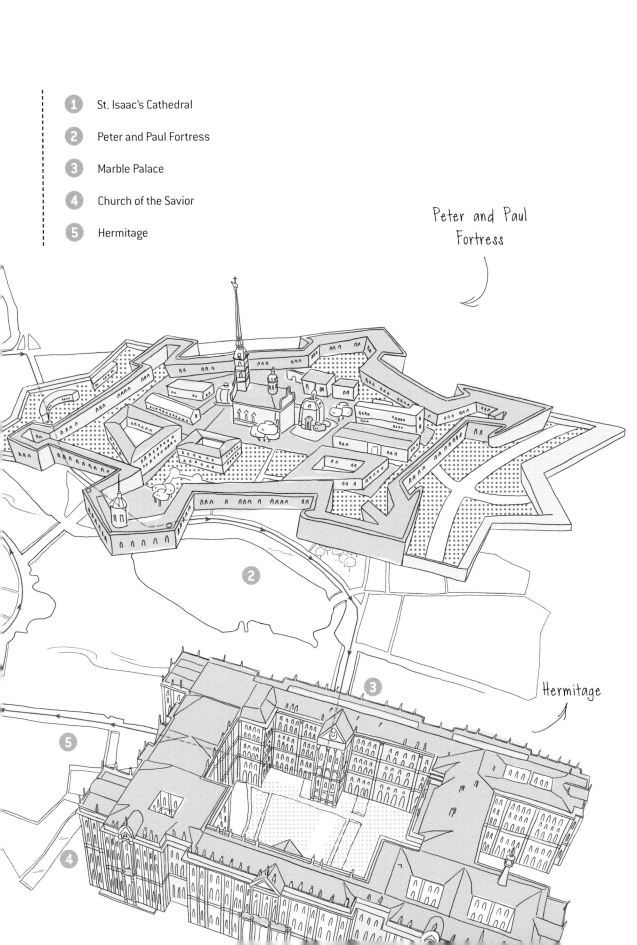

1 St. Isaac's Cathedral

2 Peter and Paul Fortress

3 Marble Palace

4 Church of the Savior

5 Hermitage

Peter and Paul
Fortress

Hermitage

ENDORPHINS

- -

After a tough workout, the feeling of exhaustion leads many runners to wonder (even just for a second) whether all the hard work is worth it. Then, as all runners will testify, as soon as you're in the shower the tiredness gives way to a pleasant sense of well-being that leaves you satisfied with how you performed and looking forward to another session.

- -

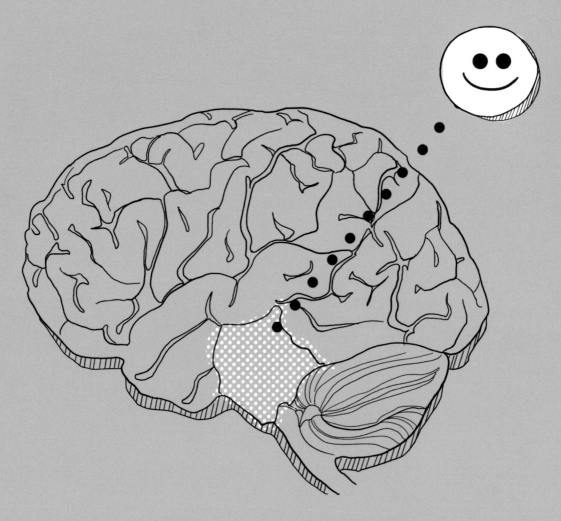

WHAT ARE ENDORPHINS?

Endorphins are chemical substances produced by our nervous system, responsible, among other things, for blocking the perception of pain. During running, as well as other forms of physical activity, the release of endorphins by the brain produces effects similar to those of natural opiates, improving our mood and reducing our sense of tiredness.

RUNNER'S HIGH

Recent neuroscientific studies seem to confirm what every runner knows from experience, in other words the direct link between prolonged physical exertion and what is generally referred to as "runner's high." Physical exercise is thought to produce biochemical effects on the brain that elevate mood.

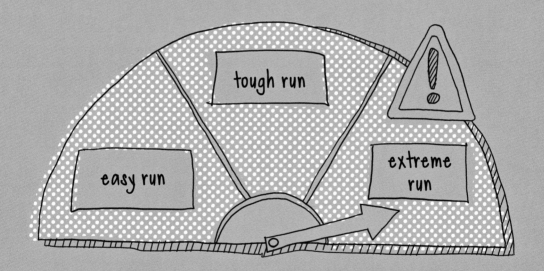

DON'T OVERDO IT

However pleasant these effects may be, try not to develop a compulsive attitude toward running. Especially for novice runners, there is a risk that this will lead to a sort of addiction. In a scene from the film *Burn After Reading*, a slightly paranoid George Clooney says desperately: "I am depressed. I gotta exercise. I haven't run in three days." Well don't let yourself get like that. Enough is enough, as the saying goes.

IN FLIGHT
FROM THE CITY

Val Venosta, Alto Adige. Almost Austria, or almost Switzerland, if you prefer. There are at least three good reasons for running the Giro del Lago di Resia: the first is that it takes place in July, when the heat and the humidity make running in the city heavy going. The second is that the distance—just over 15 kilometers—is not impossible, at least for most runners. And the third is the stunning scenery, which will definitely reinvigorate your spirits. Then there is the steeple that emerges from the lake, an iconic sight and the tangible sign of a dramatic moment in the life of the local community, when the entire town was submerged to create an artificial lake. As for the race itself, the kindness and efficiency of the organizers is something you will never forget. I could give you a fourth reason, something to do with the post-race party in the evening, but I'll let you have the pleasure of discovering it for yourself.

Opposite:
The race, which attracts over 3,000 runners every year, starts and finishes opposite the historic Romanesque bell tower of Curon: submerged in 1950, it is an iconic sight as well as a symbol for the local community.

On pages 134—135:
The course, mainly on road, follows the shoreline of the artificial lake of Resia for a total distance of 15.3 kilometers, including a stretch along the dam.

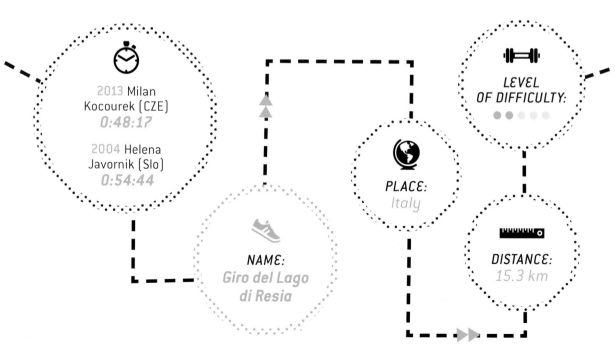

2013 Milan Kocourek (CZE)
0:48:17

2004 Helena Javornik (Slo)
0:54:44

NAME:
Giro del Lago di Resia

PLACE:
Italy

LEVEL OF DIFFICULTY:

DISTANCE:
15.3 km

The Giro del Lago di Resia follows the shore of the lake, sometimes passing through woods, for a total distance of 15.3 kilometers, run mostly on cycle tracks. The start and finish are at Curon Venosta, near the historic submerged steeple, which in many ways is the symbol of the race. There are five start waves, a few minutes apart, based on predicted times. The course, partly on road and partly on cycle tracks, is incredibly scenic. The first part, toward San Valentino and across the dam, is fairly straight. After five kilometers you reach the opposite shore, and here the course winds along some undulating sections and

RESIA

Bell Tower of Curon

a couple of climbs, then it's all flat as far as Resia, at kilometer 13, where you get a great view of the imposing Ortles glacier. Enjoy the last two kilometers or so, and store these stunning views in your memory for when you get back to running in the city.

1 Ortles (view from Resia)

2 Bell Tower of Curon

CURON

Ortles

A FEW COMMON RUNNING INJURIES
(AND HOW TO PREVENT THEM)

Sooner or later, every runner will come down with an injury. Sometimes it's just a case of transient aches, sometimes of severe, full-blown injuries. Remembering that with structural or chronic problems you should always see a specialist, here's how to recognize some of the most common injuries, and a few tips on how to deal with them.

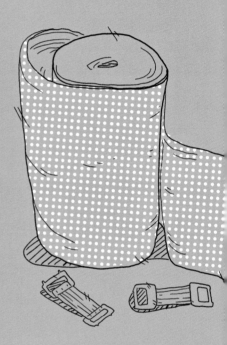

PLANTAR FASCIITIS

This is an inflammation that affects the bottom of the heel or specific areas of the arch, especially in runners with very low or very high arches. Remember that with every step the foot absorbs several times our body weight. So it's not surprising that this is one of the most common running injuries.

TREATMENT AND PREVENTION Rest, cut down on mileage, choose softer terrains, do core-building exercises, and make sure your shoes are still in good shape. Overpronators and supinators should choose suitable shoes. To relieve the pain, use ice, and to speed up recovery roll a tennis ball under your foot for a few minutes every day.

ACHILLES TENDINITIS

The Achilles tendon connects the calf muscles to the back of the heel. Inflammation can take two forms: insertional, which involves the lower portion of the heel, and noninsertional, which involves degeneration of the fibers in the middle portion of the tendon. Prolonged stress can even lead to rupture. The main symptom is severe pain.

TREATMENT AND PREVENTION Apply ice, rest, do stretching under the supervision of a sports medicine doctor, and make sure you're using the right shoes. To aid recovery, swimming or biking can be useful, as well as physiotherapy.

RUNNER'S KNEE

The pain is felt in the area of the patella, especially after intense workouts. It is usually caused by incorrect posture or overpronation.

TREATMENT AND PREVENTION Rest until the inflammation disappears, then do exercises to strengthen the hip and glute muscles. For a time you should also reduce your mileage.

IT BAND SYNDROME

Iliotibial band syndrome affects the band of fascia on the outside of the knee, and is caused by the band rubbing on the femur. A sharp pain sets in soon after you start running, though it generally disappears at rest.

TREATMENT AND PREVENTION Apply ice, make sure that your shoes are not too light for your weight, avoid uneven surfaces, and work on your running form.

STRETCHING, A USER'S GUIDE

Opinions about stretching differ, even among experts. Some claim it should be done before exercise, others that it should be done immediately afterwards, or even the next day. According to Dr. Sergio Migliorini, a specialist in sports medicine, "You should always warm up before stretching exercises because the increase in temperature reduces the viscosity of the muscle fibers. It can be done after a workout, or before a workout as long as it is preceded by at least 10 minutes of running." How should stretching be done? "The exercises must be done properly," explains Dr. Migliorini, "by gradually and slowly stretching the muscles to the limits of your range of motion, without causing pain. You should also perform your whole stretching routine several times, preferably in the afternoon when the muscles are more flexible."

THE MOTHER
OF ALL RELAYS

The Hood to Coast is an almost epic running experience. All the ingredients are there. The imposing scenery in this part of the United States. And the sense of adventure. Don't believe me? Then try running on a highway in the middle of the night with trucks roaring past and just your miner's headlamp to comfort you. Then there's the team spirit: you either make it or you fail all together. While you run you feel that the fate of your teammates lies in your legs, which gives you a powerful adrenaline boost. The formula is fantastic, and at the same time a bit wicked. You live in a van for two days, following the member of the team who is running the current leg. The finish at Seaside is worth all the hard work: the whole team crosses the line together and then there is a big party with lots of entertainment on the beach.

Opposite:
Typically wild Oregon scenery along the coast of the Pacific Ocean. The Hood to Coast passes through a variety of natural settings, from woods to mountains and finally the coast.

On pages 142–143:
The start is downhill, from Timberline Lodge on Mount Hood, which served as the exterior of the Overlook Hotel in *The Shining*.

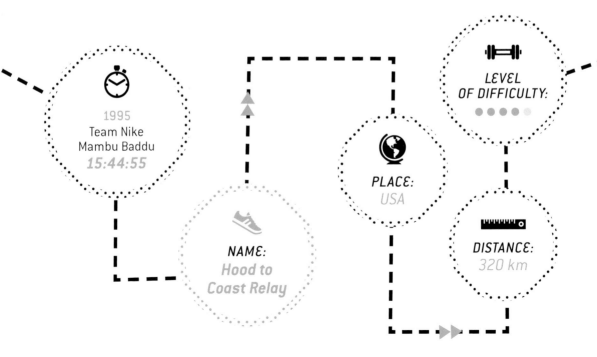

1995
Team Nike
Mambu Baddu
15:44:55

NAME:
*Hood to
Coast Relay*

PLACE:
USA

LEVEL
OF DIFFICULTY:
●●●●○

DISTANCE:
320 km

The Hood to Coast is a team relay race run in Oregon over a total distance of 199 miles, starting at Timberline Lodge on Mount Hood and finishing on the beach at Seaside on the Pacific Ocean. Each of the 1,050 teams admitted is made up of 12 runners, two drivers and two vans. The course is divided into 36 legs, from four to eight miles in length, with varying levels of incline and difficulty. During the race each runner has to cover three legs, in the same rotating sequence, passing the baton to the next runner. The six members of the team in the first van cover the first six legs, and the members of the team in the second van cover legs 7 to 12, and so on, with the vans meeting from time to time at the official exchange points. Good racing strategy thus requires a sense of direction, timing, and the adaptability needed to survive for almost two days in the confined space of the vans, with very little time to rest.

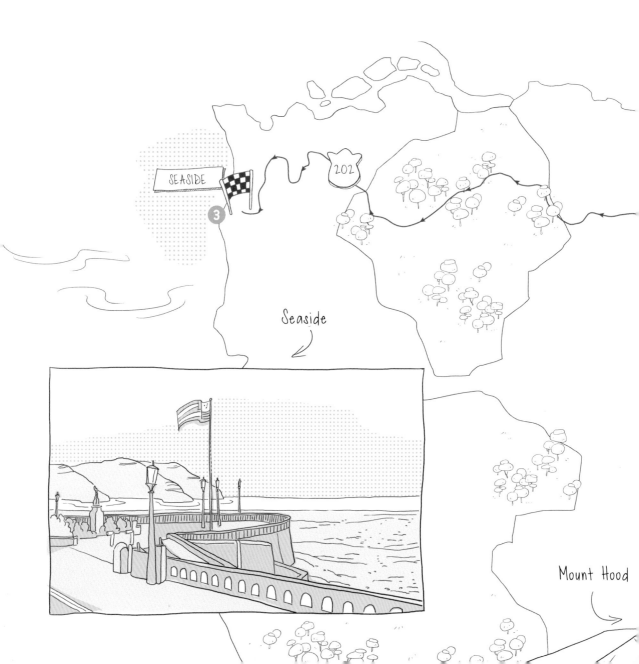

1 Mount Hood

2 Timberline Lodge

3 Seaside

Timberline Lodge

IN THE FOOTSTEPS
OF PAAVO NURMI

A modern classic, we might define it. Helsinki, a bit Swedish and a bit Russian, is fashionable, has excellent quality of life, is full of parks and cycle lanes, reconciling you to life in the city, and is surrounded by the sea. The Baltic capitals—like the neighboring Tallinn, for example—are establishing themselves increasingly as one of the beating hearts of the new Europe, rivaling cities that have always been thought of as cool. After many decades in which we associated Finland more with cutting-edge technology—Nokia, text messages, and Linus Torvald, creator of the Linux kernel —we are now realizing that art, culture, fashion, design, and haute cuisine are also part of the country's makeup. It is no coincidence that in 2012 Helsinki was elected World Design Capital. So why not do the Helsinki City Marathon? Running through the city center and over the many islands is the best way to soak up the unique atmosphere.

Opposite:
Between kilometers 22 and 23 the runners pass Kaivopuisto Park, the site of the Ursa Observatory

On pages 148–149:
The statue of Paavo Nurmi watches, quite appropriately, over the start and the finish of the race: at the 1924 Olympics in Paris the Finnish champion won five gold medals, including two (in the 1,500 m and the 5,000 m) inside an hour.

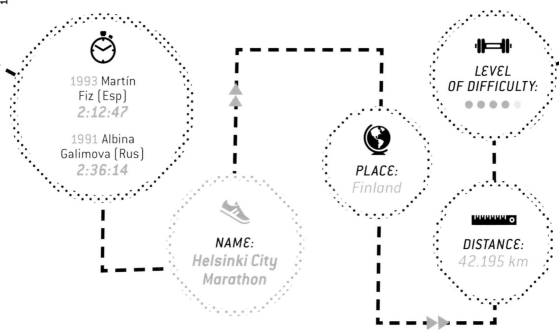

1993 Martín Fiz (Esp)
2:12:47

1991 Albina Galimova (Rus)
2:36:14

NAME:
Helsinki City Marathon

PLACE:
Finland

LEVEL OF DIFFICULTY:
●●●●○

DISTANCE:
42.195 km

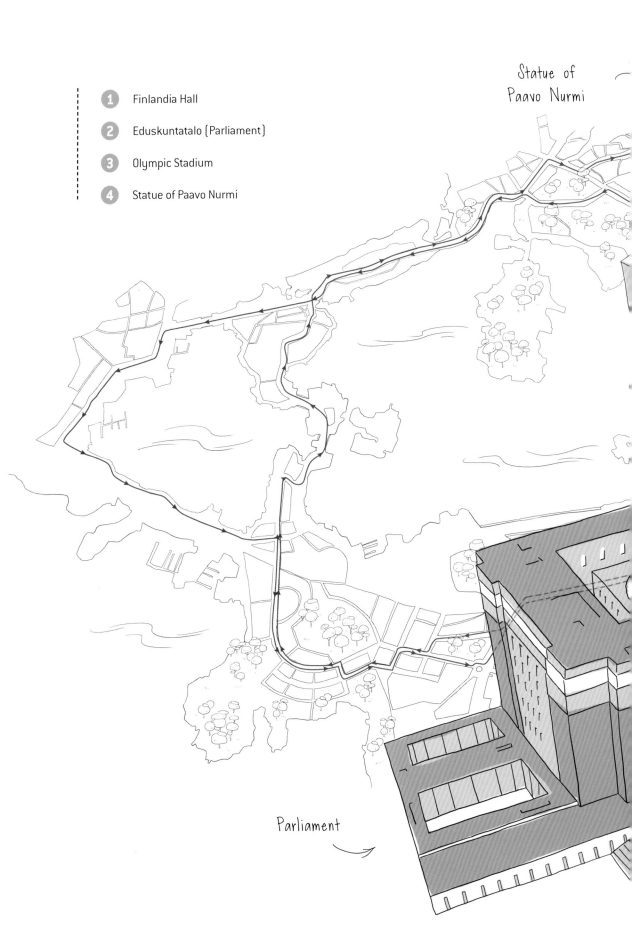

1 Finlandia Hall

2 Eduskuntatalo (Parliament)

3 Olympic Stadium

4 Statue of Paavo Nurmi

Statue of
Paavo Nurmi

Parliament

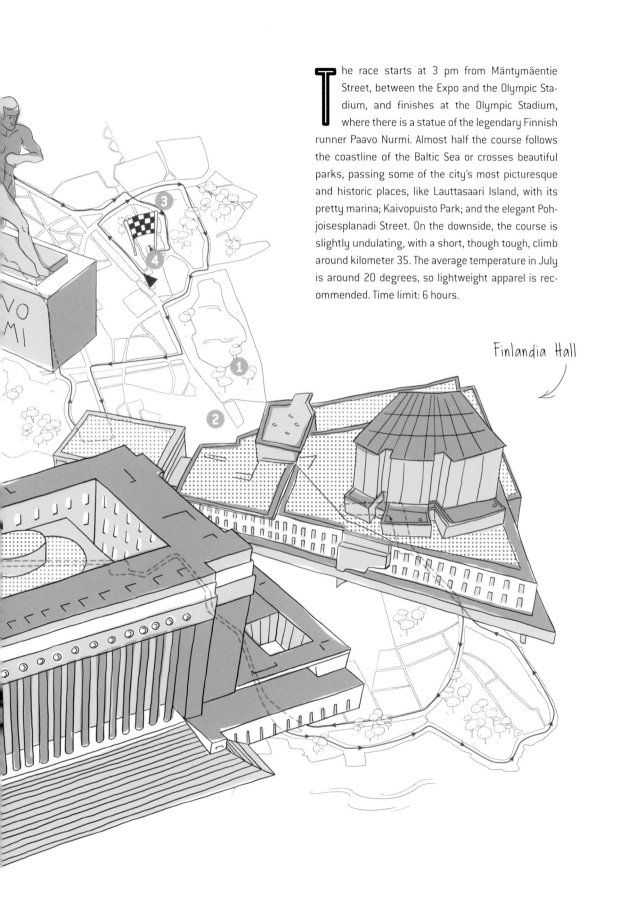

The race starts at 3 pm from Mäntymäentie Street, between the Expo and the Olympic Stadium, and finishes at the Olympic Stadium, where there is a statue of the legendary Finnish runner Paavo Nurmi. Almost half the course follows the coastline of the Baltic Sea or crosses beautiful parks, passing some of the city's most picturesque and historic places, like Lauttasaari Island, with its pretty marina; Kaivopuisto Park; and the elegant Pohjoisesplanadi Street. On the downside, the course is slightly undulating, with a short, though tough, climb around kilometer 35. The average temperature in July is around 20 degrees, so lightweight apparel is recommended. Time limit: 6 hours.

Finlandia Hall

SYDNEY
THE SURFERS'
RACE

Let's make no bones about it: the City to Surf is inspired by San Francisco's Bay to Breakers, and admits as much. But that's not necessarily a bad thing. History tells us that the idea for the race came in the 1970s when a US correspondent sent a note saying how much fun the Bay to Breakers was, and his newspaper, the *Sun Herald*, decided to organize a similar event in Sydney. The first edition, in 1971, had just over 2,000 entrants, but since then the race has grown enormously, and is now Australia's most popular fun run. In 2013, a record 83,000 runners of all levels and ages, with women outnumbering men, set off from the city center on their way to Bondi Beach. What makes the event even more interesting is its focus on fundraising: in 2013 more than $4 million was raised for over 750 charities.

Opposite:
With over 83,000 entrants, the City to Surf is Australia's biggest running race. The course record is held by Steve Meneghetti, who in 1991 covered the 14 kilometers in 0:40:03.

On pages 154–155:
The finish is at the legendary Bondi Beach: around half a mile of fine sand, a mecca for surfers and a National Heritage site since 2008.

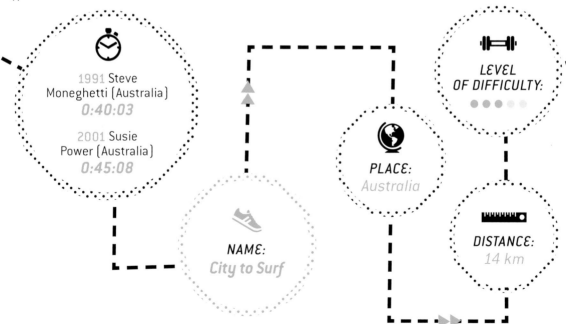

1991 Steve
Moneghetti (Australia)
0:40:03

2001 Susie
Power (Australia)
0:45:08

NAME:
City to Surf

PLACE:
Australia

LEVEL
OF DIFFICULTY:

DISTANCE:
14 km

As often happens when the weather is hot and humid, the City to Surf gets under way early, at 8 am, starting from the junction between Park Street and College Street, in the heart of the business district, and finishing 14 kilometers later at Bondi Beach, popular with surfers from all over the world. From William Street the race heads through the tunnel at King's Cross and then continues along New South Head Road toward the seafront, passing the elegant harbor at Rushcutters Bay, then Double Bay and Rose Bay. The most difficult part of the course is Heartbreak Hill at the halfway mark, a steep two-kilometer ascent up to Vaucluse, where you turn right at Old South Head Road and then left at Military Road, finally descending toward the beautiful blue water of Bondi Beach. There are six cutoff points along the course.

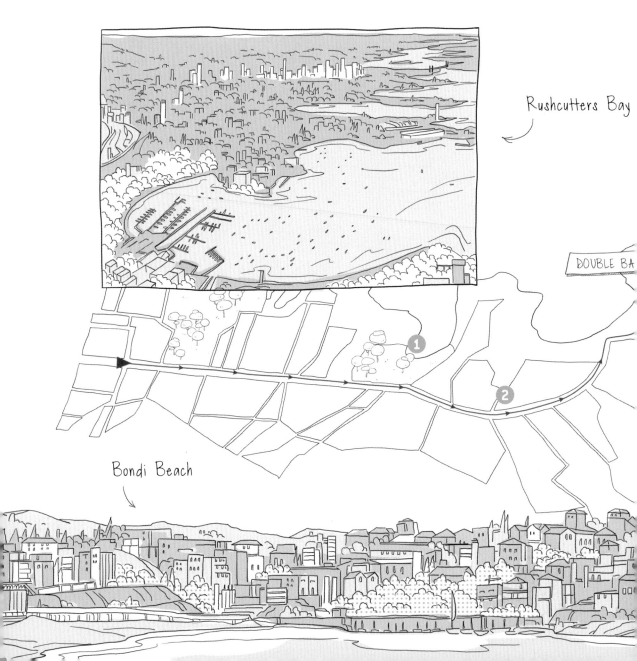

Rushcutters Bay

DOUBLE BA

Bondi Beach

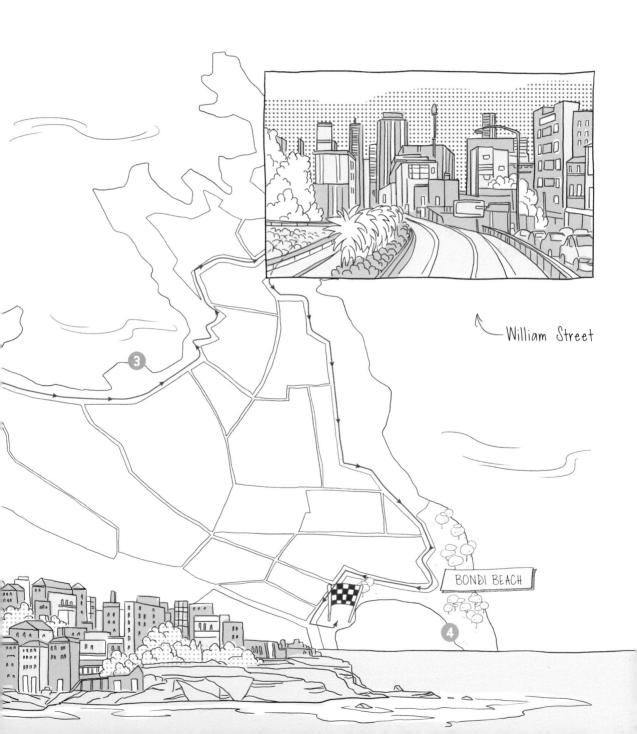

William Street

BONDI BEACH

THE TWO
SHORES
MARATHON

A French enclave in North America, as the province of Quebec is often described. And it's true: from its food to its traditions and its language, this region of Canada is proud of its links with a culture that has little to do with England. But then 200 years as a colony are bound to leave a mark. And it is precisely this very European atmosphere that makes the Quebec City Marathon so popular. Relatively young (it was first run in 1998), it now attracts almost 50,000 runners to the banks of the St. Lawrence River, and is the biggest sporting event in the region. During race weekend the locals are especially welcoming, and there is the sort of friendly atmosphere and enthusiastic support that runners always love. Add to this the province of Quebec and its amazing, varied scenery, with beautiful waterfalls and unspoilt forests, and you have another good reason to come.

Opposite:
The finish is near the Château Frontenac, a castle converted into a luxury hotel, in the city center.

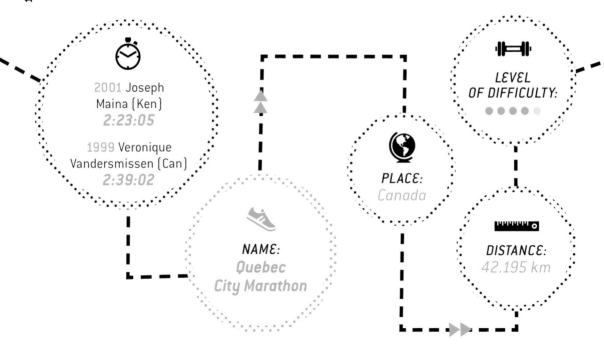

2001 Joseph Maina (Ken)
2:23:05

1999 Veronique Vandersmissen (Can)
2:39:02

NAME:
Quebec City Marathon

PLACE:
Canada

LEVEL OF DIFFICULTY:
●●●●○

DISTANCE:
42.195 km

On the morning of the race runners get to the start first by ferry to the south shore of the St. Lawrence River, then by bus to Lévis Convention Center, where the race starts at 8.30 am from Métivier Street. The finish, on the other hand, is in the Old City on the north shore, opposite the Château Frontenac Hotel, a French-style castle perched atop a tall cape overlooking the river. Most of the course follows the two shores of the river, providing some spectacular views, like the one from the Pierre Laporte Bridge, at kilometer 27, which runners cross to reach the north shore. The final part of the route passes some of the most beautiful spots in the city, like the Plaines d'Abraham, a historic area within the Battlefields Park which was the site of a battle between the French and the English in 1759; La Citadelle, a historic star-shaped fort; and the Cathedral-Basilica of Notre-Dame de Québec, rebuilt on the site of the original cathedral that dates from 1647. As far as the course profile is concerned, there is a downhill section between kilometers 10 and 11, and some undulating hills between kilometers 23 and 30. One unusual feature of the race is that unlike other marathons the kilometer markers are placed in reverse order, indicating the remaining distance to the finish line, a sort of countdown that gives runners a bit of extra motivation. As well as the full marathon, there is also a half marathon and a 10k race. Time limit: 6 hours.

1 Plaines d'Abraham

2 La Citadelle

3 Hotel Château Frontenac

4 Notre-Dame de Québec

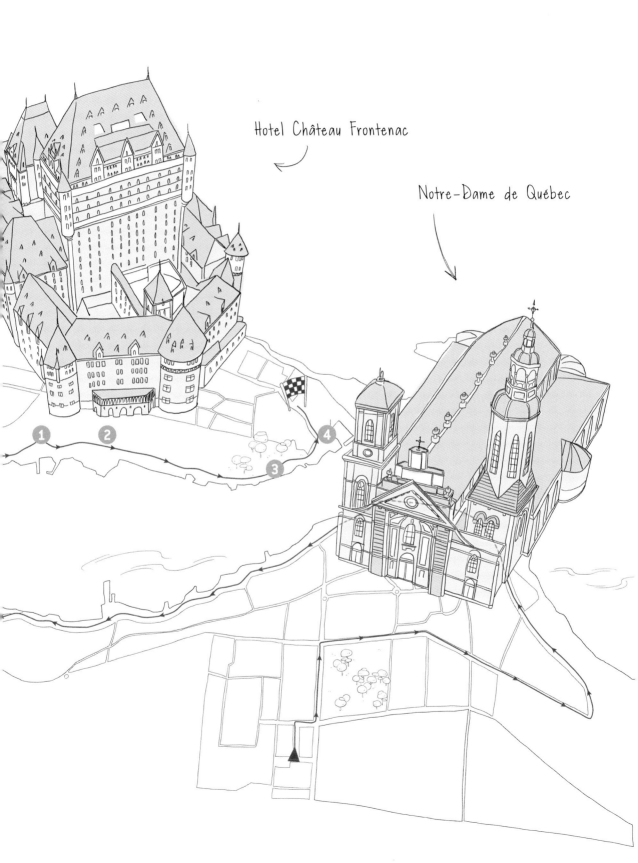

Hotel Château Frontenac

Notre-Dame de Québec

The Quebec City Marathon is also known as the Two Shores Marathon, as runners cross several times from one shore of the St. Lawrence River to the other. In the background the unmistakeable outline of the Pont de Québec.

Aerial view of La Citadelle, the military fortress located atop Cap
Diamant, built on a historic site that still houses a garrison of the
Royal 22nd Regiment.

RUNNING GADGETS

HEART RATE MONITOR

Although not indispensable, for advanced (or tech-loving) runners the heart rate monitor is a very useful tool. It consists of a chest-strap transmitter and a wrist receiver giving you real-time information on your heart rate. This allows you to train and race at the best pace. In order to be effective, your target heart rate should be based on your maximum, a rather subjective parameter that can be found by performing maximal running tests.

VIRTUAL COACH

There are many apps, for both Apple and Android, which use the accelerometer and/or the GPS module on your phone to create a personal coach who will set your training targets, send comments and compliments from your social network of running friends, and even choose suitable tunes for the various phases of your workout. A virtual coach in the palm of your hand.

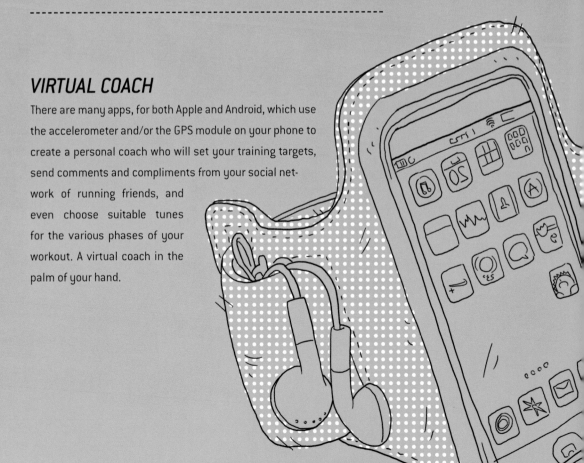

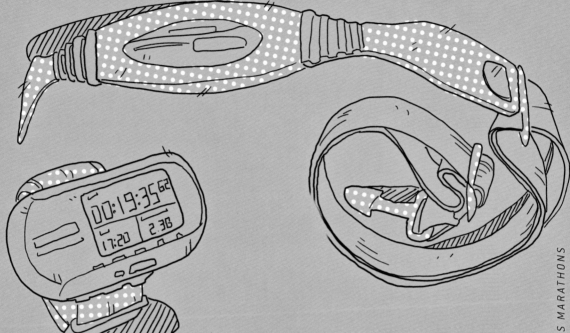

GPS WATCHES

As well as performing all the normal stopwatch functions (time, splits, etc.), GPS watches can also track distance covered, pace, calories burned, and other parameters. The data can be stored or uploaded via USB onto your computer, so you can analyze your performance or plot your routes on Google Maps.

MP3 PLAYERS

Whether or not to listen to music while running is a subject of heated debate: for some people, especially solo runners, it's the norm, while people who run with others generally prefer to remain "unplugged". It is worth pointing out that for safety reasons the use of iPods is increasingly discoraged (or even banned) in races. Apart from this, there is no doubt that music can be a motivational force. If you do use an iPod, save the upbeat tunes on your playlist for the final part of your workout. This will give you an extra boost when tiredness begins to set in.

THE LONELINESS
OF THE LONG-DISTANCE
RUNNER

There are moments in the life of a runner that are great to share with others, like the big-city marathons with tens of thousands of participants and huge crowds lining the streets. And then there are sensations that should be experienced in complete solitude, to paraphrase the title of the famous novel by Alan Sillitoe. In the experience of running alone—a long, exhausting ascent, or the smell of wet earth in a deserted park in the pouring rain—there is a special kind of satisfaction, something that belongs to us alone that the rest of the world knows nothing about. From this point of view, an event like Runiceland, a trail race through breathtaking scenery, is a wonderful opportunity. Along the course there are little glacial lakes in the craters of extinct volcanoes; imposing glaciers, each a subtly different shade of blue; and beaches of black sand, to be discovered without any fuss, without any cheering crowds. This is the most personal, contemplative side of running. Which is at least as wonderful as finishing in Central Park.

Opposite:
The Skógafoss waterfall, the start of the third stage of the 2013 edition.

On pages 168–169:
The Landmannalaugar region, where runners complete a full marathon in the lunar landscape of the volcanic desert, in the highland of Iceland.

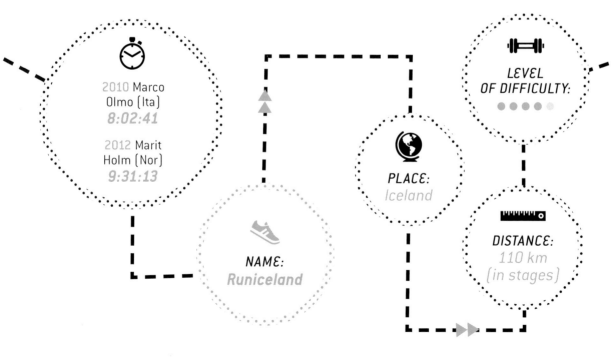

2010 Marco Olmo (Ita)
8:02:41

2012 Marit Holm (Nor)
9:31:13

LEVEL OF DIFFICULTY:
● ● ● ● ○

PLACE:
Iceland

NAME:
Runiceland

DISTANCE:
*110 km
(in stages)*

STAGE 5

STAGE 4

STAGE 3

5

4

3

2

Dyrhólaey

R uniceland is a trail race run over several days, over a total of 110 kilometers. Five stages, with varying distances and elevations, allow athletes of all levels to run in a natural environment that is nothing short of spectacular. The program of the race, which for logistical reasons is limited to around 40 runners a year, was created with the help of Marco Olmo, a living legend of extreme running. The toughest stage is probably the third, run over full marathon distance with considerable variations in elevation. The final ranking is drawn up on the basis of the sum of the times of the five stages, with a separate ranking for runners who choose to run the last 10 kilometers of the second, fourth, and fifth stages. The small number of participants means that the atmosphere is friendly and relaxed, and also makes it possible to organize sightseeing, walking, and other activities during the afternoons that follow the shorter stages.

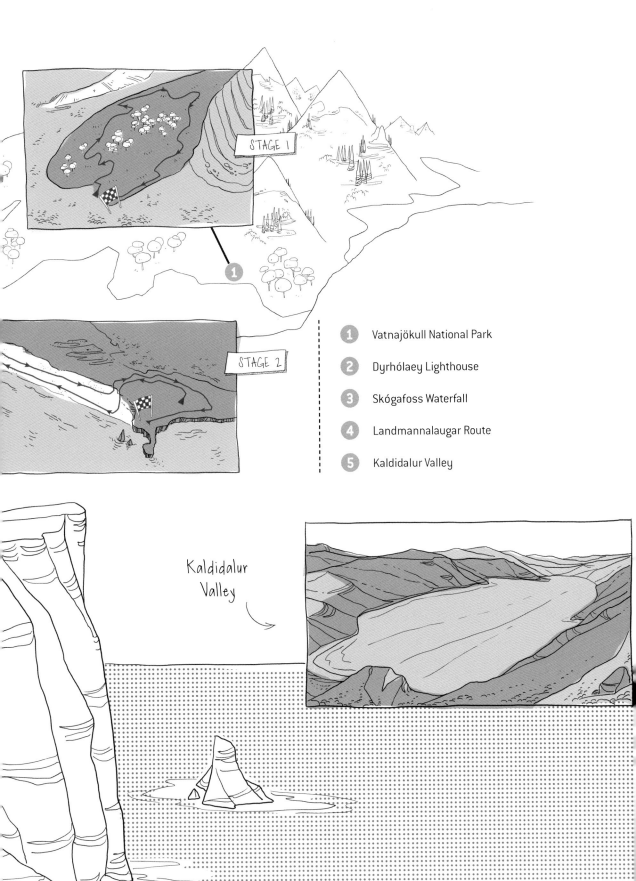

STAGE 1

STAGE 2

1 Vatnajökull National Park

2 Dyrhólaey Lighthouse

3 Skógafoss Waterfall

4 Landmannalaugar Route

5 Kaldidalur Valley

Kaldidalur
Valley

THE WORLD
RECORD
MARATHON

Question: is there a perfect marathon, with a spectacular course, huge crowds cheering you on from start to finish, great organization, and flat, uncongested roads? Answer: yes, there is—the Berlin Marathon. Runners know it well, which is why 40,000 people flock here every year. The city is full of historic sites, some of them connected to recent history, which for us Europeans means the division of Germany and then the fall of the Berlin Wall. The atmosphere you breathe as you run along the wide streets and the enthusiastic support along the route help to push you toward the fast time you've always wanted to achieve. But it's not just about times. However your race goes, running in Berlin is an unforgettable experience that will make up for all your sacrifices. Knowing that it is one of the World Marathon Majors just confirms what we all knew: the Berlin Marathon is as good as you can get.

Opposite:
30 September 2012, the final meters of the 38th edition of the Berlin Marathon. On the left the winner, Geoffrey Mutai (Kenya), with a time of 2:04:15, one second ahead of his fellow countryman Dennis Kimetto, who two years later, again in Berlin, would set a new world record of 2:02:57.

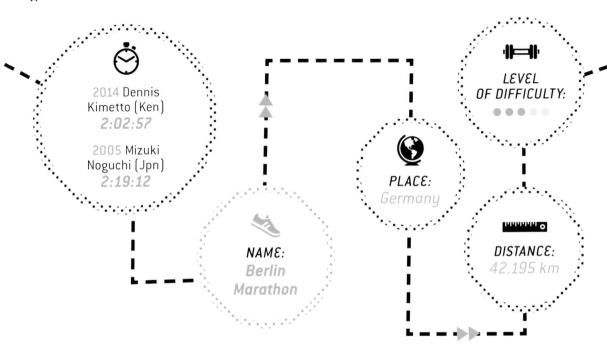

2014 Dennis Kimetto (Ken)
2:02:57

2005 Mizuki Noguchi (Jpn)
2:19:12

NAME:
Berlin Marathon

PLACE:
Germany

LEVEL OF DIFFICULTY:
●●●●○

DISTANCE:
42.195 km

Berlin is one of the fastest courses in the world, at least among the big international marathons. It is no coincidence that the most marathon world records have been set here. The race starts in three waves at 8.45 am from the Strasse des 17. Juni, between the Brandenburg Gate and the Victory Column, and finishes in the same area after completing a loop through the most important sites in the city: from the Reichstag to Potsdamer Platz and the Fernsehturm. The flat, fast course might tempt you to push too hard, especially in the first half of the race when you still feel fresh, hoping to put "minutes in the bank" for the second half of the race. But here, more than anywhere else, you need to plan a race strategy based on even pacing, holding your energy back until you reach the half-marathon mark. The difference between a great result and disappointment lies in how you manage your glycogen stores. A final word of advice. Running a marathon in September means starting your training program in July, and doing your long runs between July and August. So plan your training accordingly, especially if you live in a hot country. Time limit: 6 hours 15 minutes.

----

1. Strasse des 17. Juni

2. Fernsehturm

3. Brandenburg Gate

3. Potsdamer Platz

Brandenburg Gate

Fernsehturm

Berlin often hosts important international sports events. In the
photo, competitors in the marathon event at the 2009 Athletics
World Championships in front of the Reichstag. The race was won by
the Kenyan athlete Abel Kirui in a time of 2:06:54.

Potsdamer Platz, a symbol of German reunification after the fall of the Berlin Wall, is now a lively, modern square lined by futuristic buildings. Runners cross the square toward the end of the marathon, at around kilometer 38.

RUNNING
IN THE CITY OF
BRIDGES

A mix of Habsburg and Ottoman, Budapest has the refined elegance of a capital city with a glorious past. Its origin as two distinct cities, Buda and Pest, which were united in the late 19th century, is still visible: Buda, on the west bank of the Danube, is older, wealthier, and quieter, while Pest, its streets full of shops and tourists, is livelier, busier, and more modern. Your breath will no doubt be taken away when you see the National Museum or the Parliament, or when you walk along Andrássy Út, the famous boulevard which is now a World Heritage Site. But you're likely to be struck just as much by the famous, and very popular, thermal baths, fed by over 100 underground springs (the Széchenyi Therman Bath and the spa in the Hotel Gellert are particularly popular), and above all by Margaret Island, formerly a royal hunting reserve and now the green heart of the city, a place that seems to have been designed for runners, with its shady paths, joggers everywhere, and a running track all the way round.

Opposite:
The 19th-century Parliament Building, along the Danube embankment, seen from Buda Castle.

On pages 180–181:
A scene from the marathon. In the background is the Chain Bridge, built in 1849, the first permanent stone bridge linking the two parts of the city, Buda and Pest.

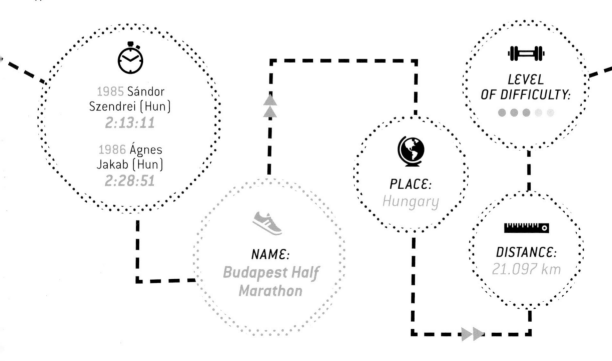

1985 Sándor Szendrei (Hun)
2:13:11

1986 Ágnes Jakab (Hun)
2:28:51

NAME:
Budapest Half Marathon

PLACE:
Hungary

LEVEL OF DIFFICULTY:
● ● ● ○ ○

DISTANCE:
21.097 km

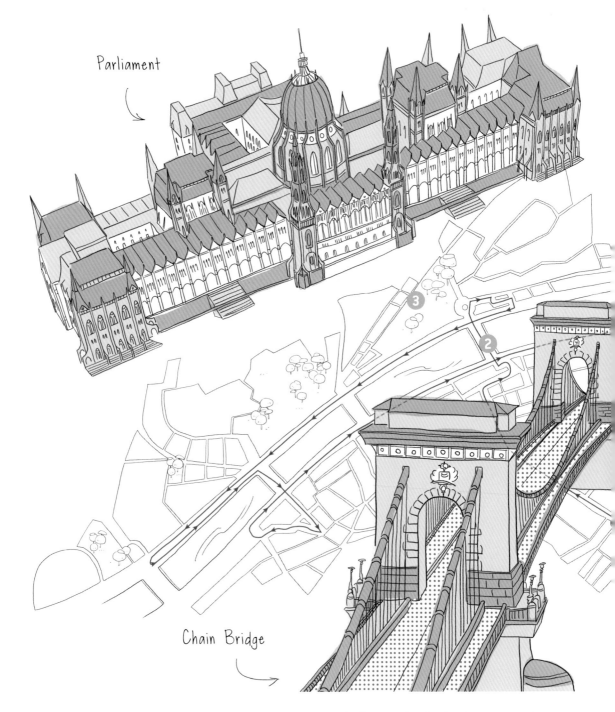

Parliament

Chain Bridge

uch of the Budapest Half Marathon is run along the banks of the Danube, with sections in both Buda and Pest, and across the bridges that take runners from one bank to the other. The race starts at 9 am very close to Heroes Square—an auspicious name for runners—built to celebrate the thousandth anniversary of the nation. After passing along Andrássy Út, the course winds through the city center with its elegant monuments, like the Opera House, the Chain Bridge,

the Parliament, the Castle of Buda, and Margaret Island. The course is mainly flat, with the exception of the bridges. The race can also be run as a relay in teams of two. In that case the first runner covers the first 11.4 kilometers, and the second runner the remaining 9.7 kilometers, with the exchange point near the Chain Bridge. Time limit: 2 hours 30 minutes, with cutoff times at kilometer 6 (43 minutes), kilometer 12 (1 hour 26 minutes) and kilometer 18 (2 hours 9 minutes).

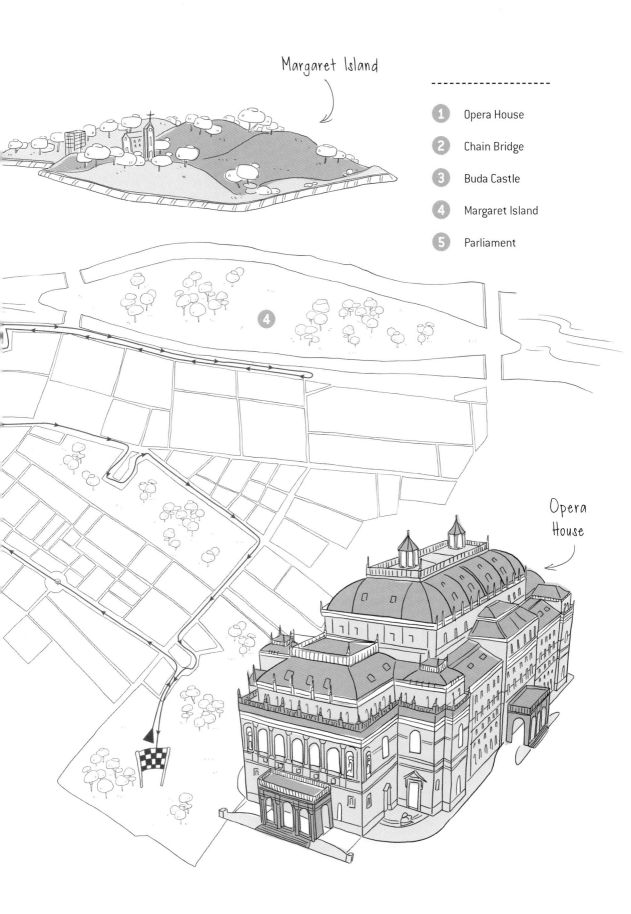

Margaret Island

1 Opera House

2 Chain Bridge

3 Buda Castle

4 Margaret Island

5 Parliament

Opera House

MOUNTAIN RUNNING

An increasing number of runners are giving up road running in favor of the much tougher challenge of trail running, or mountain running, a challenge that brings rewards such as the chance to run in stunning, often unique, scenery and to leave the city smog behind. In mountain running, as well as the usual yardsticks of running performance, distance, and time, there is a third crucial factor—altitude difference.

TRAINING TECHNIQUES

If running of any sort needs a gradual approach, then for trail running it is even more essential to take things step by step. If you are not already very fit, the first few times after a short workout you'll almost certainly feel aches and pains in muscles you didn't even know you had. This is because mountain running technique is very different from road running, and there is much greater strain on your lungs, your muscles, and your joints. If you live in a flat, urban environment, it might be almost impossible to find routes suitable for trail training. In this case, you should do strengthening exercises in the gym as well as getting on a treadmill and increasing the incline. At the weekend you should try to find trails with ascents and descents that allow a gradual approach.

TRAIL, SKYMARATHON, VERTICAL KILOMETER...

There are various forms of skyrunning, a sport that comprises a number of different mountain running disciplines, all governed by the International Skyrunning Federation (ISF), essentially on the basis of distance and altitude difference. Races range from the SkyMarathon and the Ultra SkyMarathon to the Vertical Kilometer, a race over distances of up to five kilometers with a climb of 1,000 meters.

READY FOR ALL EVENTUALITIES

Runners taking part in trail races, and even more so in ultra trail races, have to reconcile their desire to stay light with the fact that they have to be ready to cope with emergency situations and unpredictable weather conditions, which can change in the space of a few minutes, and, in longer races, to run at night. So a hydration pack, a whistle, a headlamp, a shell jacket and a mobile phone are an essential part of the runner's equipment, to the extent that they are increasingly considered obligatory in long mountain races.

OUT TO
CONQUER THE
WINDY CITY

As well as for being the third-largest city in the United States, Chicago deserves a mention for many other reasons: for its buildings and its Symphony Orchestra, because it is the city of Barack Obama and the Bulls, as well as the financial and industrial center of the Midwest. But you probably already knew this. So I'll give you two other movie-related reasons for running the Chicago Marathon, one of the six members of the World Major Marathon series. The first is that around mile 3 you run past the Richard J. Daley Center, which might not mean a lot to you, but it is the location of the final scene of *The Blues Brothers*, where hundreds of police, state troopers, and National Guardsmen join the chase. Then at around the half-marathon mark you pass Union Station, where one of the most famous scenes in cinema history was shot: the stairway shootout in *The Untouchables*, when the pram rolls down the stairs in heart-stopping slow motion. If that's not enough for you (or if you didn't grow up with 1980s movies), all you need to know is that the course is very fast and that almost two million spectators will be lining the streets to support the 45,000 runners.

Opposite:
Chicago's famous moveable bridges are not only fascinating and beautiful examples of bridge engineering, but also the way local people (and marathon runners) cross the Chicago River, which runs for miles through the city center.

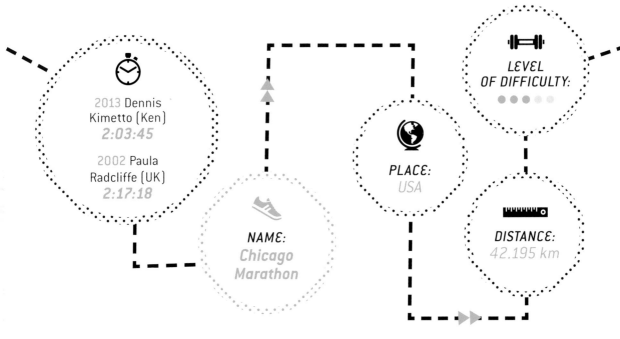

2013 Dennis
Kimetto (Ken)
2:03:45

2002 Paula
Radcliffe (UK)
2:17:18

NAME:
*Chicago
Marathon*

PLACE:
USA

LEVEL
OF DIFFICULTY:

DISTANCE:
42.195 km

The race starts near Grant Park. As in most big-city marathons,
there are several start waves based on times achieved in previous
marathons.

The imposing outline of the Willis (previously Sears) Tower. On a clear day, you can see four states from the top: Illinois, Indiana, Wisconsin, and Michigan. Runners pass the building at around the half-marathon mark.

BETWEEN THE
CÔTE D'AZUR AND
PROVENCE

Now considered a classic and recognized by the IAAF as one of the top running races in the world, the Marseille–Cassis combines the challenge of a testing course with the pleasure of running through some of the most spectacular
scenery in France, between the Côte d'Azur and Provence. The race attracts as
many as 15,000 runners and has a truly international flavor, even though the
majority of the participants, with the exception of the top runners, are French.
Be warned: if you're thinking of taking part, make sure you find out when registration opens (usually at the beginning of March), because the race is generally
fully subscribed within an hour. As for me, the registration fee is already fully
justified by the pleasure of spending the rest of the day exploring this corner of
the coastline, far from the clamor of other Côte d'Azur resorts, though no less
enchanting, and enjoying the sunset sitting outside one of the bars overlooking
the port. Sipping an excellent Cassis, of course.

Opposite:
View of Cassis from the
Route des Crêtes.

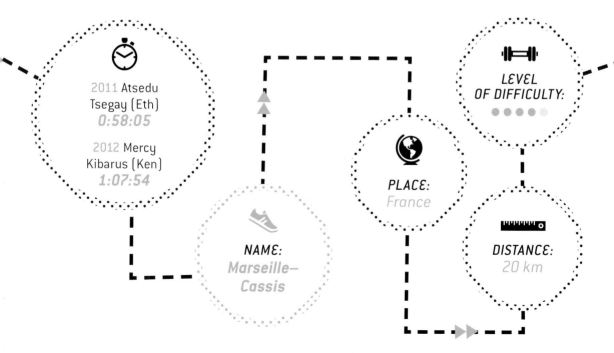

2011 Atsedu
Tsegay (Eth)
0:58:05

2012 Mercy
Kibarus (Ken)
1:07:54

NAME:
*Marseille–
Cassis*

PLACE:
France

LEVEL
OF DIFFICULTY:

DISTANCE:
20 km

The race starts at 9.30 am near the Vélodrome Stadium in Boulevard Michelet (home of the local football team Olympique de Marseille) and finishes at the port of Cassis, covering a distance of 20 kilometers, not quite a half marathon. As you leave the city the course, entirely closed to traffic, begins to wind uphill: the first half of the race is a continuous climb up to the Col de la Gineste (327 meters), which you reach between kilometers 9 and 10. You are now on the Massif des Calanques, limestone formations produced over millions of years. After the Col de la Gineste you start to descend, and in this stretch, too, there are spectacular views of Cassis and its picturesque port. At this time of year the climate is generally mild, and it's not too hot. But if you get a particularly humid day, don't worry: the tradition is that after the race all the runners take a refreshing dip in the sea. Time limit: 3 hours.

MARSEILLE

Boulevard Michelet

Col de la Gineste

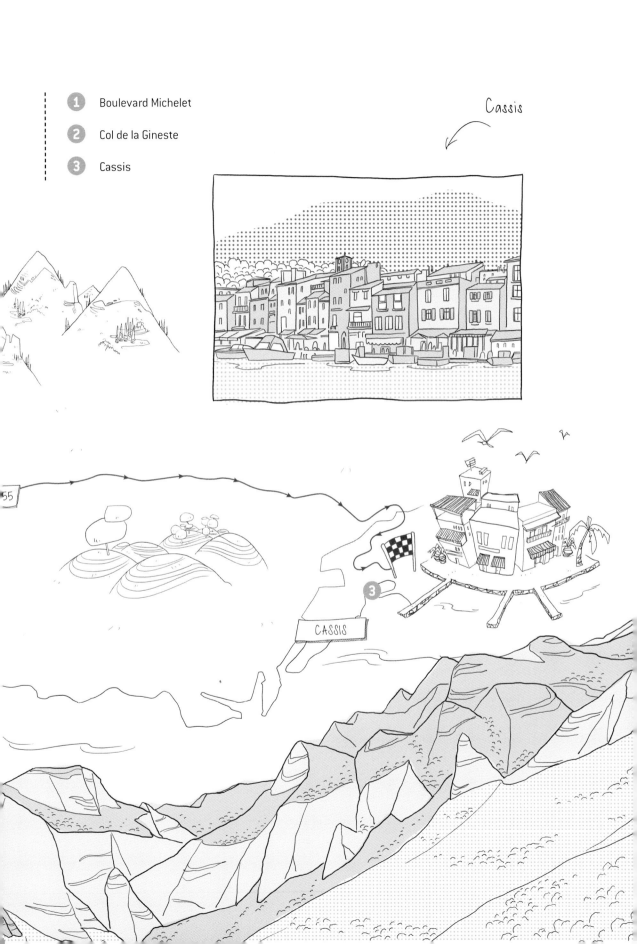

1 Boulevard Michelet

2 Col de la Gineste

3 Cassis

Cassis

CASSIS

In the last edition, over 15,000 runners set off from Boulevard
Michelet in Marseilles. In the first edition, in 1979, there were 700
entrants.

A fine view of the city of Marseille. The race was founded by a group of friends with the support of a local sports club, SCO Sainte-Marguerite.

CAN RUNNING HELP YOU
LOSE WEIGHT?

Losing weight, or at least not putting on weight, is one of the most frequent reasons for taking up the sport and at the same time one of its most pleasing effects. It's true, if you want to lose weight, running is hard to beat, provided you don't give credence to some common misconceptions, first of all the idea that losing weight always means eliminating fat...

THE RIGHT COMBINATION

Always consider running as part of a healthy lifestyle that includes correct eating habits and a nutrient diet. Make sure that the balance between what you eat and drink and what you burn is always negative. Since running has a permanent effect on your physical shape, it must become a regular part of your weekly routine and not an occasional "escape route" for shedding a few pounds. If you're a bit overweight, remember that to achieve noticeable results it takes anything between a few weeks and a few months, during which you need to run regularly, several times a week. Bear in mind that the increase in muscle mass resulting from physical activity might initially make it seem (when you get on the scale) that you're not losing weight.

DON'T BE OBSESSED
WITH THE SCALE

If you weigh yourself straight after a workout (especially an intense workout) you'll probably notice a substantial weight loss. Don't celebrate too soon: it's mainly due to fluid loss, which you will soon replace. And don't try to accelerate weight loss by not eating: if you don't eat enough, and well, the weight loss may be caused by a reduction in lean mass (your muscles) and not in fat.

HOW MUCH DO I HAVE TO RUN TO GET BACK INTO SHAPE?

The first thing to know is that everybody is different. Having said that, according to Prof. Enrico Arcelli, a specialist in sports medicine and dietology, if you are overweight you need to run an average of six kilometers a day, in other words 42 kilometers (a whole marathon!) a week. This might seem a lot, he explains, but it is possible. You can also run much less, as long as you follow a balanced diet, like the Zone diet, at the same time.

FAST OR SLOW?

According to Prof. Arcelli, the widespread belief that in order to burn more fat you have to run slowly is mistaken: "The ideal thing is to run as fast as you can without getting out of breath. Consumption depends on how many kilometers you run. And if you run at a very slow pace it takes much longer."

DON'T TAKE IN MORE CALORIES THAN YOU NEED

One common mistake among runners is to overestimate how many calories they actually burn, so they think they can (or even should) eat a large amount of carbs, or feel free (because they are running) to binge on junk food, fizzy drinks, and so on. As I mentioned in the "running gadgets" section, the latest running watches can measure how many calories you burn. In any case, try not to overeat.

DON'T GIVE UP

Running is undoubtedly one of the most effective calorie-burning sports; but don't expect miracles. For example, if you are genetically predisposed to putting on belly fat, that's where it will be difficult to lose weight, and even if you include ab exercises in your routine it might take a long time. In a way, it's like a battle in which running, diet, cross-training (biking, swimming, etc.), and an appropriate exercise routine are all on your side. So don't give up, and you'll start to see some real progress.

THE CALL
OF THE
BIG APPLE

If marathon running is now a burgeoning fashion rather than a niche sport, much is due to the appeal of the physical and mental challenge that it involves. And if there is one race which evokes this myth more than any other, it has to be the New York Marathon, with its unrivaled backdrop of visual, cultural, and cinematic references. It matters little that New York is not the easiest of courses (the slight incline on First Avenue can make your legs turn to lead), nor the oldest (a record that belongs to Boston), or that you have to cough up a small fortune just to take part: in the collective imagination this race is still the most appealing, the snapshot everyone wants in their album of running memories. If you can say "I've done New York" it's like the proof of a special status, a trophy to be shown to the world, a feather in your cap. I'm not absolutely sure it's a good thing, but the fact remains that it's something you have to do at least once in your life. If only for the unique opportunity to visit all five "boroughs" of a city which is the world's greatest melting-pot of cultures.

Opposite:
Among its merits, the New York City Marathon also covers all five city boroughs. Here runners pass through Queens, with the Chrysler Building visible in the background.

On pages 202–203:
Staten Island, where the race starts. After a long wait at Fort Wadsworth (a former military installation), runners set off from Verrazzano Bridge, which literally shakes beneath their feet.

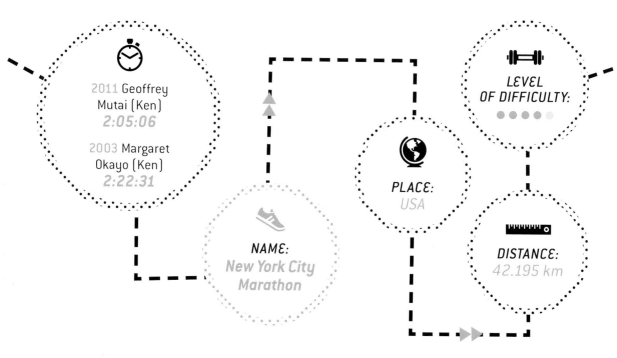

2011 Geoffrey Mutai (Ken)
2:05:06

2003 Margaret Okayo (Ken)
2:22:31

NAME:
New York City Marathon

PLACE:
USA

LEVEL OF DIFFICULTY:
●●●●●

DISTANCE:
42.195 km

Start on Staten Island, in four waves. First mile uphill on Verrazzano Bridge, with a river of runners around you that will probably slow you down. But don't worry, you'll be able to make up time on the long, wide roads through Brooklyn and then Queens. This is the flattest part of the course, up to the half-marathon mark on Pulaski Bridge. After crossing Queensborough Bridge, at mile 15, you turn onto First Avenue with three or four miles of slight hills that explain why the native Americans called this area "Manna-hata," or "Island of Many Hills". Mentally, this is the toughest part of the course, because it's easy to get dispirited on what seems like an endless straight stretch, with "the wall" looming at around mile 20. Fortunately the next section is flat, through the Bronx and onto Fifth Avenue with Central Park on your right. You think it's almost over, but there are still three miles or so to go and a couple of taxing hills. Past the Reservoir, you enter the park, and if you've trained properly you'll be passing plenty of people who have started to walk. At the southern end of the park, you proceed along Central Park South before reentering the park at Columbus Circle: just a few hundred yards to go, and finally the finish line is in sight. Time limit: 8 hours. A final word of advice: the support from the New York crowds is quite amazing, often almost moving. But it can be a double-edged sword: a few high fives are all very well, but zig-zagging the whole course will cost you dear. So don't let the high-fiving get out of hand!

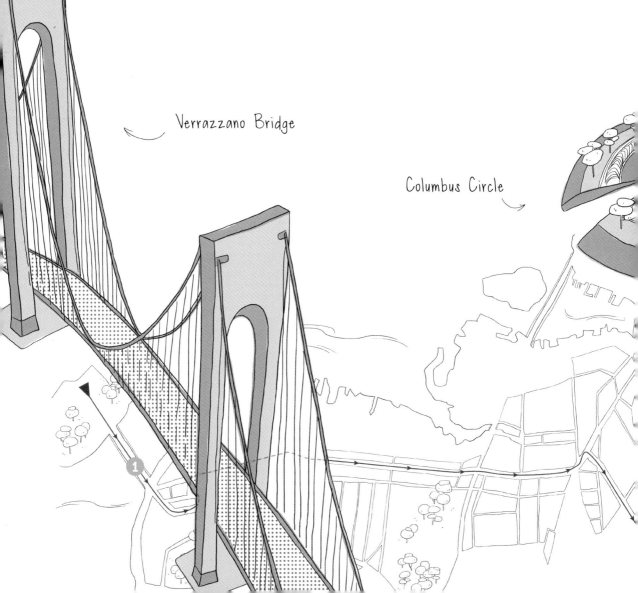

Verrazzano Bridge

Columbus Circle

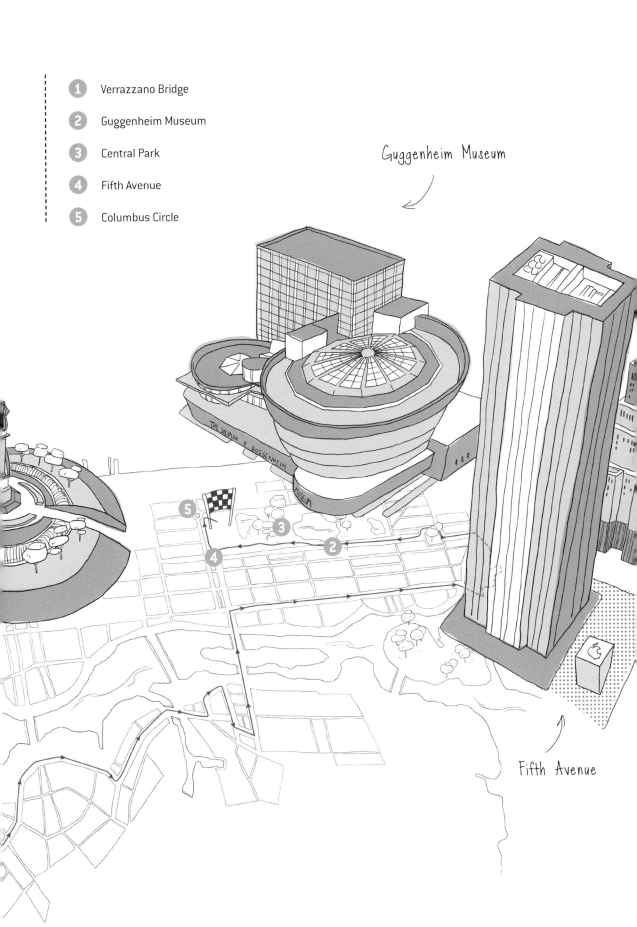

1 Verrazzano Bridge
2 Guggenheim Museum
3 Central Park
4 Fifth Avenue
5 Columbus Circle

Guggenheim Museum

Fifth Avenue

FIVE COMMONSENSE TIPS FOR YOUR
FIRST MARATHON

RESIST TEMPTATIONS

If the marathon is in a city you've never visited before—and especially if you've come with family or friends—you'll probably be tempted to spend the day before the race sightseeing or shopping. Even if these activities may not seem to be tiring, they might turn out to be a fatal error, affecting your performance on the big day. If you don't believe me, ask someone who has run the New York Marathon what happens if you spend the whole of Saturday walking up and down Fifth Avenue.

DON'T USE NEW SHOES

Running in shoes you've never worn before might turn your first marathon experience into a nightmare. Make sure you "run them in" first, even wearing them for a few days when you're not running. And on the subject of shoes, if you're traveling by plane make sure you keep them in your hand luggage, together with your marathon registration card. If the worst comes to the worst, at least you won't lose your race-day essentials.

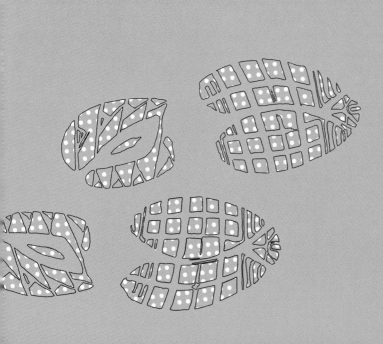

DON'T EXPERIMENT WITH ANY NEW FOODS FOR YOUR RACE-DAY BREAKFAST

And avoid any food or drinks that might cause you stomach problems (milk, for example, gives many people an upset stomach). Have a substantial breakfast, but don't overdo it. If you've eaten well and haven't wasted energy in the last few days before the race, you won't need to eat more than you normally would. If it helps to make you feel more relaxed, as well as or instead of the hotel breakfast you could eat food that you've brought from home (as long as you can take it on the plane) and that you know you can digest easily.

DON'T SET OFF TOO QUICKLY

After the starter's gun—especially if it's your first marathon—it's easy to be overwhelmed by the excited (and almost epic) atmosphere at the start. Very few runners manage to resist the temptation to set off at full pace, forgetting that they have 26 long miles to go. Set off slowly, and watch out for runners rushing past you in the first few hundred meters (if you want to avoid the risk of being accidentally tripped up, try running with your arms stretched out behind you), then try to find your own pace, perhaps by settling in behind the pacemakers for your target time. If you start out too fast you'll usually pay for it in the second half of the race, when you'll almost certainly have to slow down. Take my advice: save your energy up to the half-marathon mark and then try to keep up a steady pace, holding something back for the last few miles.

TRY NOT TO LET YOURSELF GET DISTRACTED

Enjoy the race, the spectators, the cheers, and the bands along the course, but remember that you might regret all the zig-zagging to give high fives when you need all the physical and mental energy you can summon up in the last few miles. Watch out for uneven paving, cobbles and tramlines in city centers. Focus on where you are putting your feet. The refreshment stations can also be a bit hazardous, especially in big-city marathons, where the road soon gets covered in bottles, gels, paper cups, and water. Stop running and walk for a few meters as you drink, and then try to set off again in the middle of the road, where it will be less slippery.

26.2 MILES
IN PARADISE

The Honolulu Marathon is a perfect case that reveals a lot about runners' minds. Let me explain: what is it that drives a human being without self-destructive tendencies to fly for two days in cramped conditions, land in a beautiful destination but suffering from serious jet-lag, get up at half past two in the morning to make it to the starting line of a race that begins in the dark, in which as well as running 26 miles he will have to face suffocating heat and humidity? The answer is that for a marathon runner the challenge of running in these extremely uncomfortable conditions is motivation in itself. Add to that the allure of Hawaii and the Island of Oahu (the fact that *Magnum, P.I.* was filmed here is enough for me), and the spectacle of the sun rising as you run, and you will understand why 30,000 people decide to take part in the race every year, making it the third-largest American marathon. So, aloha!

Opposite:
The sponge and drinking stations are important when running a marathon in hot, humid conditions. To avoid the worst of the heat, the Honolulu Marathon starts at 5.30 am.

On pages 210–211: Diamond Head and Waikiki Beach are among Hawaii's most recognizable landmarks. At the summit of the extinct volcanic crater you can visit bunkers, military fortifications, and artillery stations dating back to the First World War.

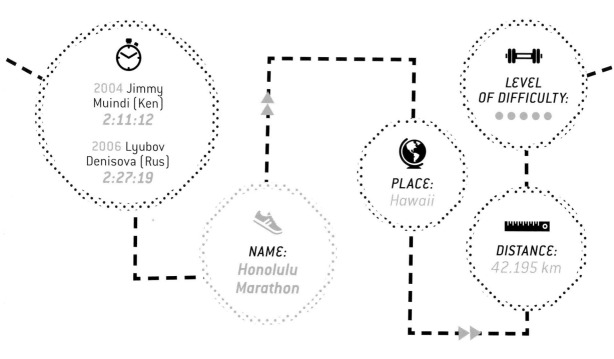

2004 Jimmy Muindi (Ken)
2:11:12

2006 Lyubov Denisova (Rus)
2:27:19

LEVEL OF DIFFICULTY:

PLACE:
Hawaii

NAME:
Honolulu Marathon

DISTANCE:
42.195 km

The race starts at 5.30 am near Ala Moana Beach Park. And since not many marathons kick off with a fireworks display, it's not unusual for many runners (especially the Japanese, who come here in large numbers) to stop and take photos. The course is quite flat, with the exception of two sections around Diamond Head with fairly steep inclines: the first from mile 6 and the second from mile 24. The main difficulty, however, is the temperature (already about 20 degrees at the start) and especially the humidity, which you have to cope with right from the start. Fortunately, there are aid stations every two to three miles, and wet sponges and water sprinklers to help you cool down. A word of advice: drink at regular intervals, but don't overdo it, or you might experience stomach problems. The good news is that most of the course is close to the sea, with fantastic views of places like Waikiki Beach, one of the most popular

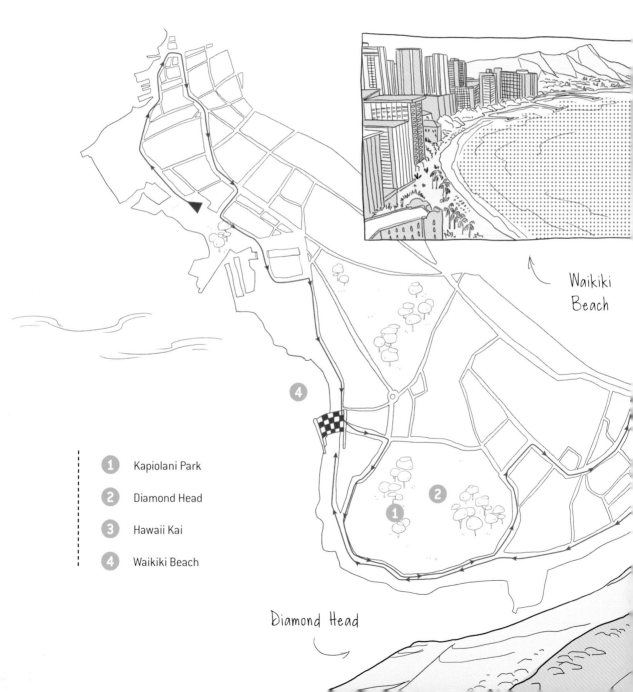

Waikiki Beach

1 Kapiolani Park

2 Diamond Head

3 Hawaii Kai

4 Waikiki Beach

Diamond Head

tourist spots in Hawaii, or Diamond Head, a volcanic crater with a unique, iconic profile. Between miles 16 and 17 the course turns back toward the start, first through the wealthy residential area of Hawaii Kai and then through the even more exclusive Kahala before reaching the finish line in Kapiolani Park, just in front of Waikiki Beach, where you get a lovely shell necklace together with your medal. No time limit.

Hawaii Kai

RACING
INTO THE
NEW YEAR

Ten kilometers. If you think true runners are only interested in the marathon, you're wrong. Running shorter distances, from the half marathon down, can be very stimulating, and can also be a good test if you're working your way up to the "ultimate goal," the marathon. And in the case of the San Silvestre Vallecana there are also a few incentives that have little to do with performances and goals. For example, it's an original way to bring in the New Year (or to end the year "on the right foot," perhaps), and it's also a great way to see the sights of Madrid, a city which is always a pleasure to visit, but which is particularly attractive during the festive season, with a beautiful display of Christmas lights all over the center. The race, too, is a joyous, colorful celebration, with 40,000 happy runners filling the streets. So enjoy every meter, and then let the party begin!

Opposite:
Plaza de Cibeles owes its name to the beautiful fountain dedicated to the goddess Cybele. It is delimited by several historic buildings, including the famous Cybele Palace, which in 2007 became the Madrid City Hall.

On pages 216–217:
The Atocha Railway Station houses a covered tropical garden with over 260 plant species. The runners pass the station between kilometers 6 and 7.

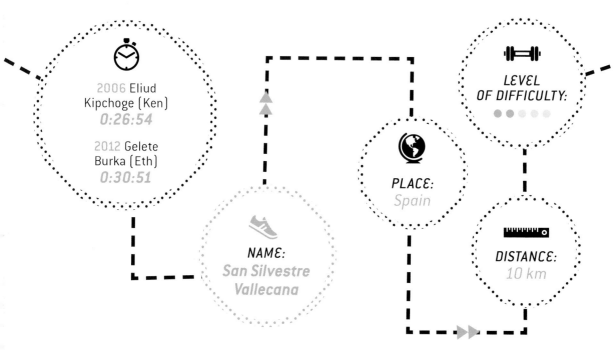

2006 Eliud Kipchoge (Ken)
0:26:54

2012 Gelete Burka (Eth)
0:30:51

LEVEL OF DIFFICULTY:

PLACE:
Spain

NAME:
San Silvestre Vallecana

DISTANCE:
10 km

The start of the San Silvestre Vallecana is on Avenida de Concha Espina, close to the legendary Santiago Bernabéu stadium. The event includes a fun run ("popular"), open to everyone, and an elite race ("internacional") for runners with fast times: under 38 minutes for men, and under 45 minutes for women. Because of the large number of entrants, the start is in four waves, every 15 minutes from 5.30 pm, with the third wave reserved for women only. The elite race, which attracts a top international field, starts at 7.55 pm. The course takes in part of the center, passing Plaza de Cibeles and the Prado, then the botanical garden and Atocha Station. The fun run finishes in Calle Candilejas, while the elite race finishes in the nearby Vallecas stadium.

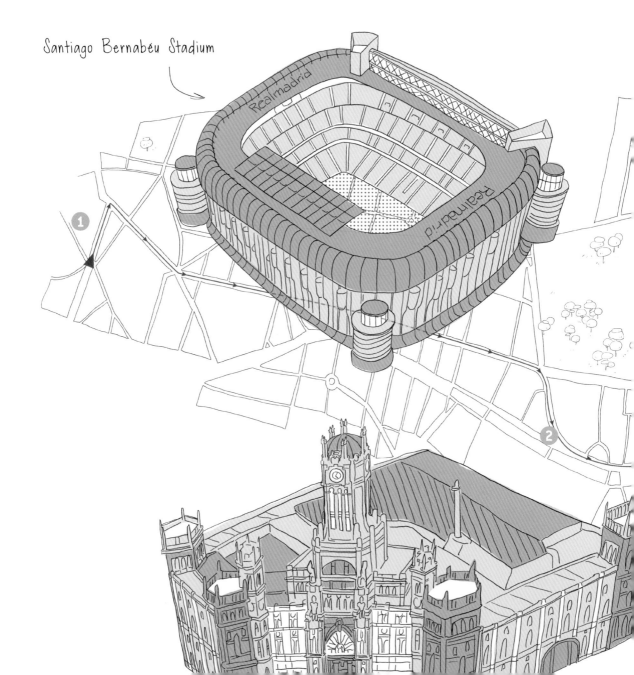

Santiago Bernabéu Stadium

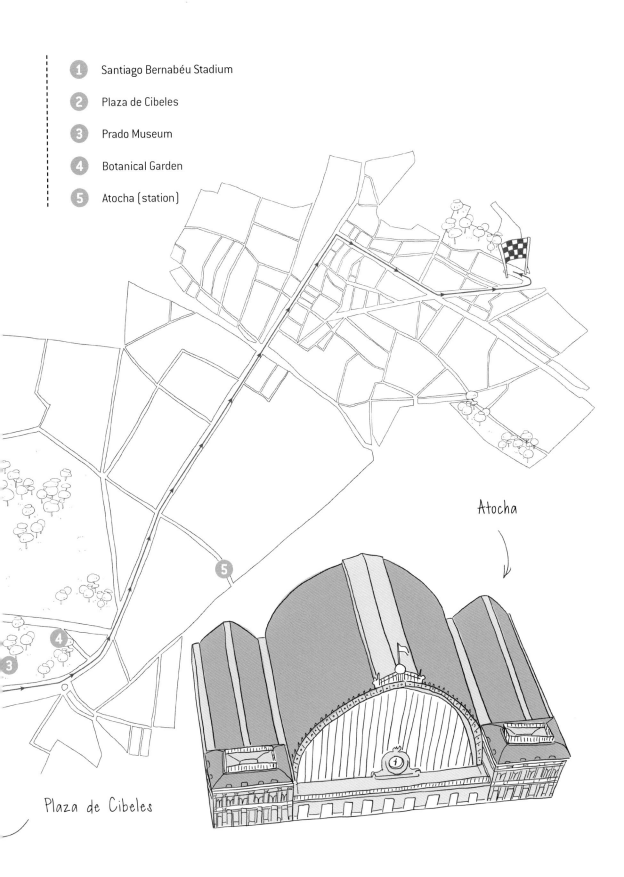

1 Santiago Bernabéu Stadium

2 Plaza de Cibeles

3 Prado Museum

4 Botanical Garden

5 Atocha (station)

Atocha

Plaza de Cibeles

PHOTO CREDITS

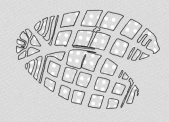